Armoured Vehicles of the First Gulf War
1990–91

AF087636

Finlay Reynolds

MILITARY VEHICLES AND ARTILLERY SERIES, VOLUME 9

Front cover image: Abrams firepower: Prior to deploying to the Middle East, the US Army spent weeks test-firing its tanks. The M1A1 Abrams proved its value during the 1991 Gulf War and after the war, it was upgraded to MIA2. (US DoD)

Title page image: The Bradley Armoured Fighting Vehicle pictured in the desert sands of Kuwait in 1991. The US Army deployed 2,200 to the Gulf War. It is often described as the ultimate 'battlefield taxi'. (US DoD)

Back cover image: The Abrams tank is regarded as the best tank in the world following its success in Gulf War One. The US Army's Abrams tanks spearheaded the invasion of Iraq in 2003. (US DoD)

Published by Key Books
An imprint of Key Publishing Ltd
PO Box 100
Stamford
Lincs PE9 1XQ

www.keypublishing.com

The right of Finlay Reynolds to be identified as the author of this book has been asserted in accordance with the Copyright, Designs and Patents Act 1988 Sections 77 and 78.

Copyright © Finlay Reynolds, 2024

ISBN 978 1 80282 869 6

All rights reserved. Reproduction in whole or in part in any form whatsoever or by any means is strictly prohibited without the prior permission of the Publisher.

Typeset by SJmagic DESIGN SERVICES, India.

Contents

Introduction 4

Chapter 1 United States of America 5

Chapter 2 United Kingdom 34

Chapter 3 France 58

Chapter 4 Iraq 70

Chapter 5 The Gulf States 110

Introduction

The Gulf War of 1991 saw the biggest deployment of armoured vehicles since World War Two. Often referred to as Operation *Desert Storm* or the First Gulf War, it took place after Saddam Hussein's Iraqi forces invaded and occupied the neighbouring oil state of Kuwait in early August 1990.

The Iraqi President had borrowed millions of dollars from several Gulf States to fund his war with Iran, which took place between 1980 and 1988. When that war ended, the dictator called on the Arab states to cancel the debts owed by his administration. He argued that the loans should be considered payments to Iraq for protecting the Arabian Peninsula from Iranian expansionism, but his appeals went unanswered.

By early 1990, Iraq's economy was close to collapse and Saddam Hussein's Baghdad administration needed to generate revenue. The conflict with Teheran had been very costly, and the country needed to repay its loans. Saddam saw Kuwait as the answer. The Kingdom was a wealthy country; its revenue generated through oil production.

Prior to the Iraqi invasion, Kuwait had 104 billion barrels of oil in reserve and sat among the ten richest states in the world. Today, it is the fifth richest. Concerned that Iraq would attack other Arab countries, Saudi Arabia and Egypt called on the United States and other Western nations to intervene. At the time, Iraq's army was the fifth largest in the world, with 5,500 main battle tanks and more than 10,000 armoured vehicles – almost all of which were Soviet era. Iraq refused to leave Kuwait, forcing an Arab coalition, heavily supported by Western forces, to eject the invaders from Kuwait. The 1991 Gulf War was unique in that US President George Bush (Senior) agreed on the proviso that any military Coalition that ejected Iraq, should be Arab led. Arab coalition members who deployed armour in 1991 included Kuwait, Saudi Arabia, Egypt and Syria. They were supported by the United States, the UK and France. After months of negotiations, the United Nations passed resolution 678, which approved the use of force to remove Iraq forces from Kuwait. The United States and a multi-national coalition headed by Arab nations now assembled a military force in the desert in readiness to act if Saddam failed to withdraw by January 1991.

In total, 42 countries supported Operation *Desert Storm* with a huge force of armoured vehicles. This book takes a look at the nations that contributed tanks and armoured vehicles, including tracked armoured personnel carriers (APCs) and special vehicles to identify any chemical threat. Iraq deployed more than 26 different armoured vehicles. Egypt provided the largest regional force, but the main fighting formation of Coalition forces was the US VII Corps and the British. This was a war that proved the significance of the tank, which had first emerged 75 years earlier on 15 September 1916 on the battlefield at Somme in World War One.

Finlay Reynolds

Chapter 1
United States of America

The US Army embraced the 'tank' in both world wars and quickly developed the platform into the 'king of the battlefield'. The United States deployed tanks to Vietnam and in Panama, but the Gulf War was the first experience of tank warfare for the US since 1945 and the baptism of fire for its new Abrams main battle tank (MBT). The tank battles of 1991 highlighted the importance of modern tanks, packed with technology, which allowed the crews to fire while on the move. The Abrams delivered speed and firepower in an assault that took the Iraqis by surprise and decisively defeated a battle-hardened and dangerous enemy. The tank's modern technology allowed the US to identify enemy targets and fire while advancing towards the Iraqis. Across the desert, many Iraqi tanks sat in static positions, except at the Battle of Norfolk, which saw Iraq's elite tank units facing the US. The battle involved three epic encounters – known as 73 Easting, Medina Ridge and Fright Night. Here the US went muzzle-to-muzzle with Iraqi tanks. The enemy had thousands of serviceable Soviet-era tanks, but nothing to match the firepower of the Abrams and Bradley fighting vehicles.

M1 ABRAMS – Main Battle Tank

The Abrams M1A1 is an icon of military hardware, regarded by many as the best main battle tank ever developed. The Gulf War was the first combat deployment for the Abrams. The tank received a firepower upgrade and improved nuclear, biological and chemical warfare (NBC) protection before deploying to the Middle East in late 1990. It is a third-generation main battle tank designed by Chrysler Defence – later renamed General Dynamics Land Systems. Heavy armour brings huge firepower to a battle as well as speed; these key factors make the Abrams a formidable offensive weapon platform. Its gas turbine engines allow this MBT to reach speeds of 42mph across surface roads on which it has a range of more than 260 miles. However, it is thirsty and required regular fuel stops during the 1991 Gulf War.

The Abrams was developed from the failed MBT-70 project that intended to replace the M60 tank, which entered service in 1960 and was due to be retired, but was retained by the US Marines Corps (USMC) and used in Operation *Desert Storm*. The M1A1 was designed for modern armoured ground warfare and is currently one of the heaviest tanks in service, at close to 68 tonnes. Early versions of the

The Abrams M1A1 is an icon of military hardware and regarded by many as the best main battle tank (MBT) ever developed. Heavy armour, and especially the Abrams, bring huge firepower to a battle as well as speed; these key factors make the Abrams a formidable offensive weapon platform. (US DoD)

Above left: The interior of an M1A1 Abrams MBT provided much more room for the crew than previous platforms such as the M60 and Sheridan, which were very cramped. (US DoD)

Above right: The gunner can view the target through a number of systems prior to engagement. Many systems have been upgraded since the 1991 Gulf War. (US DoD)

Before deploying Abrams tanks, crews test-fired their weapons systems in a series of exercises. The Gulf War was the first combat deployment for the Abrams. (US DoD)

With a top speed of 42mph and its precision-firing system, the Abrams outgunned and outmanoeuvred the Iraqi tanks, which were becoming obsolete. (US DoD)

M1 were equipped with a 105mm M68 cannon, but later versions were fitted with a 120mm L/44 gun from manufacturer Rheinmetall known as the M256. After decades of development, the tank entered service in 1980 and was quickly deployed to Europe where it impressed NATO colleagues with its manoeuvrability and speed.

The tank's armour is a composition of a Rolled Homogeneous Armour (RHA) – steel plates around protective material – and later the M1A1 was also upgraded with Chobham armour. This dual combination of Chobham armour and RHA could stop almost any missile launched at the Abrams – although the US-produced Hellfire missiles was able to penetrate its armour. To evade enemy forces, the crew can launch a smoke screen to hide the tank from enemy fire, while the NBC protection system is based around a special airtight liner and clean, conditioned air system, which includes a radiological warning device, and a chemical alert.

Right: Tanks were loaded aboard US Navy ships for transportation to the Gulf and later their return to the United States, in a journey that took several weeks. (US DoD)

Below: The US Army shipped several hundred tanks to the Middle East. The crews reversed their guns to allow the Main Battle Tanks (MBTs) to be parked inside the cargo vessels. (US DoD)

An armoured recovery unit, known as the M88A2 Hercules, sits with Abrams and other vehicles after being unloaded. It was introduced in 1991 to support the heavy Abrams. (US DoD)

The design of the Abrams took crew safety seriously; there is more room inside it than other tanks, although it is still 'tight' for space. A halon automatic fire extinguisher system is housed within the tank to suppress any incidents. The ammunition for the main gun is housed in the rear of the turret behind blast doors that open and close automatically when a spent cartridge is ejected. Fuel and ammunition are stored securely in armoured compartments with blowout panels to prevent the ammunition from exploding, if damaged. These units also contain the crew's protective jackets and face masks.

M1 Abrams Specification	
Model	M1A1
Manufacturer	General Dynamics Land Systems
Country	United States
Year	1980–to present
Engine	1500hp gas turbine engine
Fuel	Diesel
Protection	Chobham armour and uranium plates
Top Speed	42mph on road (67km/h)
Range	265 miles (426km)
Crew Capacity	Four
Length	32ft
Width	12ft
Height	8ft
Armament	120mm M256 smoothbore
Secondary Armament	One coaxial 7.62mm, one top turret 7.62mm machine gun and one 12.7mm anti-aircraft machine gun
Weight	67 tonnes
Service Branch	US Army	USMC

The M1A1 was superior to Iraq's Soviet-era T-55 and T-62 tanks, as well as Iraqi-assembled Russian T-72s and locally produced copies – although the tanks' fuel economy created logistical challenges. (US DoD)

Tank crews take a break at a forward-operating base in the desert. More Abrams tanks can be seen under camouflaged nets in the rear of the picture. (US DoD)

Above left: Crews were trained to carry out maintenance on their tanks, including changing wheels and repairing tracks. (US DoD)

Above right: Major maintenance such as engine changes were carried out by specialist engineering teams equipped with recovery platforms that could lift the engine and, if needed, tow the Abrams. (US DoD)

In the rear echelons, mechanics repaired major damage including fitting new wheels and changing gearboxes. (US DoD)

Above: Abrams M1A1s provide flank protection to Coalition personnel carriers as they advanced. (US DoD)

Left: Two Abrams tanks push a bomb-damaged Iraqi main battle tank off the highway just after Coalition forces liberated Kuwait. (US DoD)

M60 – Main Battle Tank

The M60 tank entered service in 1959 and was used in the 1991 Gulf War by the US Marines. This veteran tank had reached full operational capability by December 1960 and remained in service for 30 years. It was a second-generation main battle tank operated by the United States Army and had been developed from the M48 Patton, America's first-generation main battle tank, incorporating many of its characteristics in the initial design. It has occasionally been unofficially categorised as a Patton tank family member.

Chrysler Defence Plant in Newark began an initial production line in June 1959 after the contract was approved in April of that year. Due to the Soviet Union's tank developments in the late 1950s and the delays in developing the armour and an upgraded turret design, the original model of the M60 series was eventually manufactured as a quick-fix modification of the M48. The final M60 was equipped with a 105mm, M68 main gun with a bore evacuator – which extracts lingering gases from fired ammunition in the crew space – positioned towards the centre of the tube. A total of 57 rounds were held in the M48 adopted turret. A further nine rounds were concealed below the loader on the left side of the turret tray. The M60 was designed to use revolutionary composite armour – consisting of layers of different materials including metals, plastics, ceramics, and air. This armour could withstand bigger blasts than

Above left: The M60, which had entered service in 1959 was deployed in the 1991 Gulf War by the US Marines. It had previously undergone an upgrade and in Operation *Desert Storm* had improved armour. (DPL)

Above right: An M60 fitted with reactive armour prior to being deployed to the Middle East in 1990, where it waited for its role in Operation *Desert Storm* in early 1991. (US DoD)

Operation *Desert Storm* saw the largest deployment of the M60 tank – seen here on a transporter – which was deployed by the US Marines. After the 1991 conflict, the M60s were retired. (US DoD)

The M60 had been deployed to Germany in 1962 to take part in NATO war games during the Cold War (1947–91) alongside German, French and British armoured units. (DPL)

The M60 incorporated the British-designed 105mm gun as its main gun and was able to destroy any known enemy tank at the time. Its improved armour and mobility made it a lethal platform. (DPL)

traditional all-steel rolled homogeneous armour. Despite being able to withstand initial impacts better than steel, the armour panels quickly deteriorated and needed refurbishment adding to its maintenance costs. Designers opted to go with an all-steel design, making the M60 the last American tank to have all-steel armour. When the US Army ended the manufacture of the M60 hull in 1983, it was decided to upgrade more than 5,000 older vehicles in service. This included increasing the turret armour thickness and changing the flammable hydraulic fluid in the turret for a non-flammable alternative.

The M60 tank series became America's principal main battle tank during the Cold War (1947–91), spearheading NATO war games in Europe and was often seen taking part in war games in Germany. The tank proved deadly in battle during the Gulf War, with tank crews reporting that the armour upgrade allowed it to head the advance towards Kuwait International Airport, destroying hundreds of Iraqi T-55 and T-62 tanks, including several Soviet-designed T-72s, and a number of armoured personnel carriers and vehicles. The M60 tank-on-tank combat in the Gulf War was the largest in US Marine Corps history. The M60A3 tanks used by the USMC were later replaced by the Abrams tanks and formally retired from US military service. After Operation *Desert Storm*, the US stopped using the M60 in front-line combat; those in service with the National Guard were de-commissioned in 1997.

M60 Specification	
Model	M60 | upgraded M60A1 | M60A2 | M60A3
Manufacturer	Chrysler Corporation Delaware Defence Plant
Country	United States
Year	1960, subsequently upgraded in 1962, 1974 and 1979
Engine	Continental AVDS-1790 series turbo supercharged, fuel injection 12-cylinder 750hp (559kW)
Fuel	Diesel
Protection	Cast homogeneous armour steel hull and turret with Kevlar lining
Top Speed	30mph (48km/h)
Range	310 miles (500km)
Crew Capacity	Four
Length	30ft
Width	12ft
Armament	105mm M68 rifled gun 7.62mm machine guns and .50 cal M85 heavy machine gun
Weight	51 tonnes
Service Branch	US Army | USMC

A USMC crew sleep on military cot beds, while colleagues carry out repairs to their M60 at a remote desert base. (US DoD)

An M60 fitted with mine-clearing claws. The tank, in its combat engineer role, could be fitted with a dozer blade to help clear obstacles ahead of the main tank assault. The 165mm gun allowed the crew to clear bunkers and any other potential hurdles. (US DoD)

Left: Marines from Company D, 2nd Tank Battalion US Marines (USMC) aboard an M60A1 main battle tank during a beach exercise prior to Operation *Desert Storm*. The tank is fitted with reactive armour and with an M9 bulldozer kit. (DPL)

Below: An M60 during Operation *Desert Storm* in 1991, fitted with mine-clearing equipment, heads a convoy of USMC amphibious assault carriers, often known as Amtracs. (US DoD)

M551 Sheridan – Light Tank

The light M551 Sheridan, an airborne deployable reconnaissance tank, was used by the 3rd battalion (Airborne) 73rd Armoured Cavalry Regiment in the 1991 Gulf War. It was deployed with a thermal sight upgrade and was assigned to a flank protection role, which saw crews involved in tank-on-tank combat. The Sheridan was adopted by the American Army in 1969 – it was named after General Philip Sheridan and was intended to be an effective light tank. Weighing approximately 16 tons, the M551 Sheridan's hull was constructed from aluminium alloy, while the turret was made of steel. The Sheridan was 22ft long and just over 13ft wide. Powered by a General Motors 6V53T, six-cylinder 300hp supercharged diesel engine, the Sheridan could reach road speeds of nearly 45mph. It had a cruising range of 373 miles. The Sheridan was amphibious, capable of swimming across water at a speed of 4mph. It could also be air dropped to provide fire support to airborne units.

The US Army deployed the light M551 Sheridan tank to the Gulf War – an airborne deployable reconnaissance tank, it was used by the 3rd Battalion (Airborne) 73rd Armoured Cavalry Regiment in the conflict. (US DoD)

The Sheridan benefitted from a low profile, but some crews reported the Sheridan was simply too light for the tremendous recoil that resulted from firing the main gun. (US DoD)

The key element of the new tank was the untried XM81 gun-missile launcher system capable of firing both 152mm cannon rounds and the Shillelagh missile. Unlike previous tank gun rounds that used conventional brass shell casings, the XM81 fired rounds with combustible cartridge cases. Early variants of the tank were deployed to Vietnam, which highlighted the platform's flaws, particularly its poor survivability and dependability. It was later sent to South Korea and also assigned to US battalions based in Europe. Despite the fact that there was no true substitute at the time, the Army started to phase out the Sheridan in 1978, although the 82nd Airborne Division was allowed to retain them until 1996. During the US invasion of Panama, or Operation *Just Cause*, in 1989, a total of 14 Sheridan tanks were deployed with C Company, 3/73rd of the 82nd Airborne Division, marking the Sheridan's sole combat air drop during its years of service.

Above: The M551 was small, light and fast, allowing tank crews to steam ahead in a reconnaissance role and provide screening patrols. (US DoD)

Left: A Sheridan of the 3rd Battalion 73 Airborne Armoured Cavalry arrives in the Middle East by air transport plane. The tank's limited weight made it suitable to be flown forward ahead of other forces. (US DoD).

In 1990, during Operation *Desert Shield*, Sheridan tanks were air-landed in Saudi Arabia during the early stages of the mission, before heavier armour arrived via ship. The US Army hurriedly delivered 60 M551A1 TTS variants with the thermal sight modification ready for operations. During Operation *Desert Storm*, the 3/73 Cavalry were tasked to protect the main force in a screening role and found itself engaged in combat with the Iraqis.

This was the only time Shillelagh missiles were fired in anger. In the main, their light armour and advanced age restricted them to a reconnaissance mission during *Desert Storm*.

M551 Sheridan Specification	
Model	M551 Sheridan | known as XM551 light | M551A1
Manufacturer	Cadillac Motor Company
Country	United States
Year	1969
Engine	Detroit Diesel (General Motors)
Fuel	Diesel
Protection	7039 aluminium alloy hulls, Rolled Homogeneous Steel turret
Top Speed	45mph surfaced road (72km/h)
Range	350 miles (560km)
Crew Capacity	Four
Length	21ft
Width	9ft
Height	9ft
Armament	152mm gun/missile launcher, 7.62mm machine gun, .50-calibre machine gun
Weight	17 tonnes
Service Branch	US Army

A Sheridan drives away from a C-130 Hercules having landed at a remote airstrip in a training exercise prior to being deployed to Operation *Desert Storm*. (US DOD)

The Sheridan could be dropped in a low-level tactical assault operation, during which a parachute is deployed and then pulls the tank out of the aircraft and provides enough lift to counter any damage to the M551. (US DoD)

Prior to their deployment to the Middle East, tanks were put through their paces in a series of war games to test their firing systems, crew response times and ability to evade detection. (US DoD)

Above left: An upgraded M551 pictured at a US armoured training ground prior to the Gulf War. Its high speed allowed the M551 to easily flank objectives. The Sheridan was mainly assigned to US airborne forces before being withdraw from service. (US DoD)

Above right: The low profile at the front of the tank allowed the driver a greater view; the raised centre body provided crew space. Together with the shaped turret, these elements of designer were all seen as innovative at the time. (US DoD)

M2 Bradley – Armoured Fighting Vehicle

The development of the M2 Bradley delivered enhanced protection for troops, as well as firepower and mobility. During Operation *Desert Storm*, Bradley crews destroyed more Iraqi vehicles than the Abrams M1A1 main battle tank. Of the 2,200 Bradleys sent to the Persian Gulf in 1991, 1,730 were assigned to deployed operational units while 470 were held in reserve. In total, 20 were lost, three to enemy action and 17 to friendly fire incidents; another 12 were damaged. The process to identify a future armoured personnel carrier began in 1963 but made little progress. Then, when military commanders saw the potential of the Soviet BMP vehicles, which were used by Egyptian and Syrian forces in the 1973 Yom Kippur War, they identified the need for a new platform to confront the Soviet threat in Europe.

Named after US General Omar Bradley, the vehicle's speed had to match that of the new M1 Abrams main battle tank in order for it to keep battle formation – which had been impossible with the older M113 armoured personnel carrier that the Bradley was to replace. The first Bradley fighting vehicle

During Operation *Desert Storm*, the Bradley was a formidable armoured fighting platform. Pictured here during a pause in the battle the M2 Bradley crews destroyed more Iraqi vehicles than the Abrams M1A1. Of the 2,200 Bradleys sent to the Persian Gulf in 1991, 1,730 were assigned to deployed operational units while 470 were held in reserve. (DPL)

The Bradley was delivered to the US Army in the 1980s and was shipped to Europe to take part in Cold War manoeuvres in towns across Germany (illustrated). Named after US General Omar Bradley, the vehicle's speed had to match that of the new M1 Abrams main battle tank in order for it to keep battle formation. (DPL)

entered service in late 1981 and officially replaced the ageing M113 – although the M113 remained in service. It represented a huge change from the M113 armoured personnel carrier. It was designed to carry personnel but differed markedly from the M113 in its ability to defeat armoured vehicles with its 25mm Bushmaster cannon, and defeat personnel targets using the 7.62mm coaxially mounted machine gun. Later, it also became a tank killer with the Bradley M3 upgraded tube-launched optically tracked, wire-guided (TOW) missile. The missiles, capable of destroying most tanks to a maximum range of 4,000 metres (13,000ft), can only be fired while the vehicle is stationary.

The original Bradley was improved in the 1986 variant with the TOW II. The next version was in 1988, which saw active service in Operation *Desert Storm*. The success of the vehicle during the operation brought it renewed prominence and praise for its performance.

Very fast and agile, the Bradley has a three-person crew – commander, gunner, and driver – with six fully equipped troops in the rear. Often described as 'half tank, half taxi', the Bradley is the ultimate combat taxi capable of 41mph on surface roads. The Bradley is also amphibious, and early models were equipped with a water barrier, which is fitted by the crew before entering the water. Water propulsion is provided by tracks and the Bradley can reach a maximum speed of seven knots. The Bradley demonstrated its capability in the 1990–91 conflict and went on to serve in later campaigns. Today, it remains pivotal to the US Army's mechanised infantry capability.

Left: Pictured firing at night, the Bradley force was designed to carry personnel. It differed markedly from the M113 in its ability to defeat armoured vehicles with its 25mm Bushmaster cannon, and to defeat personnel targets using the 7.62mm coaxially mounted machine gun. (US DoD)

Below: The US military spent weeks training in the desert for the assault in February 1991. Since the Gulf War upgrades have ensured that the M2 Bradley, pictured on a firing range, remains the primary armoured fighting vehicle used by the US. (US DoD)

M2 Bradley Specification	
Model	M2A1 Bradley Armoured Fighting Vehicle
Manufacturer	United Defence
Country	United States
Year	1981–95 (United Defence)
Engine	Cummins VTA-903T 8-cylinder diesel 600hp (450kW)
Fuel	Diesel
Protection	Spaced laminate armour offering 14.5mm all around protection. Hull base is 7017 aluminium
Top Speed	40mph (64km/h); 25mph off-road; 4.47/mph in water
Range	300 miles (482km)
Crew Capacity	Nine (three crew, commander, gunner, and driver), plus six passengers
Length	22ft
Width	11ft
Height	10ft
Armament	Main armament: 25mm M242 chain gun (900 rounds) 2 × TOW anti-tank missile launchers (seven missiles) Secondary armament: 7.62mm coaxial M240 machine gun
Weight	25 tonnes
Service Branch	US Army | USMC

Prior to deploying to the Gulf, Bradley crews took part in numerous 'rehearsal' exercises in which soldiers and vehicles wore electronic laser alarms – which can be seen on the soldiers' clothing. When enemy forces fired at these beacons, a 'hit' triggered an alarm to indicate the wearer had been hit. (US DoD)

Above left: The engine bay on the Bradley was designed to make access to the Cummins diesel engine easy. Routine checks were carried out by the crew. Major engine changes and overhaul was assigned to an engineering battalion. (US DoD)

Above right: The Bradley's engine is in the front and is protected from attacks by armoured panels. In deep maintenance, these panels can be removed allowing complete access to the engine bay. (US DoD)

Left: The vehicle's hydraulic rear ramp, operated from the inside, allows soldiers to quickly 'mount up' with equipment. (US DoD)

AAV7A1 AMTRAC – Amphibious Armoured Personnel Carrier

The AAV7A1 is an amphibious armoured personnel carrier, often known as the Amtrac. It entered service in 1972 as a replacement for the ageing LVTP-5, that had been in service with the USMC since the 1950s and was known as the LVTP7. In 1985, the USMC changed the designation of the LVTP7 to AAV7A1 — amphibious assault vehicle — representing a shift in emphasis away from the long-time LVT (amphibious) designation, meaning 'landing vehicle, tracked'. Without a change of a bolt or plate, the AAV7A1 was to be more of an armoured personnel carrier and less of a landing vehicle. Weighing in at 26 tons combat-loaded, and with a three-man crew, it can officially carry 21 personnel. With a road speed of 45mph, this vehicle is fully amphibious with water speeds up to 8mph. It is not as heavily armoured as the US Army's Bradley infantry fighting vehicle.

In November 1990, a large-scale amphibious exercise, with codename 'Imminent Thunder', was held near the head of the Persian Gulf. While the surface assault was cancelled, the concept created the basis of a deception plan, which left Iraq commanders thinking the Coalition would strike from the sea – they didn't.

USMC personnel pour out of the back of an Amtrac during training. In 1990–91, the USMC spent weeks training in the Kuwaiti desert. In 1985, the Marine Corps changed the designation of the LVTP7 to AAV7A1 (amphibious assault vehicle) representing a shift in emphasis from the long-time LVT (landing vehicle, tracked) designation. (US DoD)

Weighing in at 26 tons combat-loaded, and with a three-man crew, the AAV7A1 can carry 25 Marines. With a road speed of 45mph, this fully amphibious vehicle travels in water up to 8mph. The vehicle had limited armour. (US DoD)

Above left: The Amtrac is a fully amphibious vehicle, and in November 1990, a large-scale amphibious exercise, named 'Imminent Thunder,' was held near the head of the Persian Gulf. (US DoD)

Above right: The Amtrac, a tracked armoured personnel carrier (APC), performed well in the heat of desert. The aim of the Amtrac was to ferry marines safely to their objective, where they would then leave from the rear ramp and go into action. (US DoD)

The USMC deployed several variants and received much notoriety in *Desert Storm* during the liberation of Kuwait and destruction of Saddam's forces – although they proved vulnerable to Iraqi rocket attack.

AAV7A1 AMTRAC (renamed from LVTP7 in 1984 by USMC) Specification	
Model	Amphibious Armoured Personnel Carrier
Manufacturer	FMC Systems
Country	United States
Year	1972–present
Engine	Detroit Diesel/Cummins
Fuel	Diesel
Protection	45mm (1.8in) of armour plate
Top Speed	20mph off-road; 45mph on surface road (72km/h), 8mph in water
Range	300 miles (480km) – 20 nautical miles in water at sea state 5
Crew Capacity	Three crew, commander, gunner, and driver, plus 21 passengers
Length	26ft
Width	11ft
Height	11ft
Armament	MK19 40mm automatic grenade launcher, 96 rounds ready and 768 stowed 12.7mm M2HB heavy machine gun, 200 rounds ready, 1,000 stowed
Weight	29 tonnes
Service Branch	USMC

LAV-25 – Armoured Light Reconnaissance Vehicle

The LAV-25 is an eight-wheeled light armoured reconnaissance vehicle initially ordered by the USMC which was first used in combat in the invasion of Panama in 1989, before being deployed to the Persian Gulf in 1990 in preparation for the liberation of Kuwait in 1991. The LAV-25 is seen as a workhorse of the USMC, and its design is based on the Swiss Piranha series of wheeled vehicles.

It was developed in the late 1980s after the USMC sought a light armoured vehicle (LAV) that could deliver speed and protection. After development, this 15-tonne LAV entered service, being delivered in command, anti-tank, recovery and logistics roles. The USMC ordered 758 variants of what was termed the LAV-25. In 1991, the all-terrain capability of the LAV-25 appealed to the 82nd Airborne, which borrowed at least a dozen and deployed them on Operation *Desert Storm*.

The LAV-25 is essentially a highly equipped armoured personnel carrier, although it can perform a range of tasks due to its ability to move quickly, manoeuvre, and deliver firepower. LAVs can cross inland waterways, rivers and streams with the least amount of preparation since they are amphibious and can be in the water within three minutes. The vehicle is armed with a 25mm chain gun, which can effectively engage armoured and thin-skinned vehicles. It can also be equipped with additional weapons, such as anti-tank missiles or machine guns, depending on the mission requirements.

Above left: The LAV-25 is an eight-wheeled light armoured reconnaissance vehicle initially ordered by the USMC, which was first used in combat in the invasion of Panama in 1989, before being deployed to the Persian Gulf in 1990 in preparation for the liberation of Kuwait in 1991. (US DoD)

Above right: In 1991, the all-terrain capability of the LAV 25 appealed to the 82nd Airborne, which borrowed at least a dozen and deployed them on Operation *Desert Storm*. (US DoD)

The LAVs were transported to the Middle East by ship just as they had been when participating in exercises in the UK and Europe. On operations, the driver's position was locked down and vision was through small optics, which provided a 180-degree field of sight. (US DoD)

Above left: Maintaining machinery such as thermal image cameras and night-vision equipment was part of routine checks on the LAV carried out by crew members. (US DoD)

Above right: A LAV-25 pictured in the desert. The eight-wheeled vehicle often carried two spare tyres and strapped bags and rations to the side of the vehicle. (US DoD)

Below: After the success in helping the Arab states liberate Kuwait from Iraqi forces, returning US Army formations took part in a parade in Washington, which included units equipped with the LAV 25. (US DoD)

During the Battle of Khafji, in the Gulf War in 1991, the LAV-25 played a significant role in repelling Iraqi forces and securing the town of Khafji. Its mobility allowed fast response and manoeuvrability, enabling the marines to quickly adapt to changing battlefield conditions. The battle for Khafji saw the USMC involved in heavy fighting and it reported losing at least two of its lightly armoured vehicles. The LAV-25's capabilities and effectiveness made it a game-changer in the Gulf War.

LAV 25 Specification	
Model	Armoured Reconnaissance Vehicle
Manufacturer	General Motors	General Dynamics Land Systems
Country	United States/Canada
Year	1983–present
Engine	Detroit Diesel 6V53T 300hp
Fuel	Diesel
Protection	Welded steel
Top Speed	62mph (100km/h), 6mph in water
Range	410 miles (480km)
Crew Capacity	Three crew, commander, gunner, and driver, plus six passengers
Length	21ft
Width	8ft
Height	9ft
Armament	M242 Bushmaster 25mm chain gun plus two 7.62mm machine guns
Weight	13 tonnes
Service Branch	United States Marine Corps. Twelve loaned to 82nd AB

M113 – Armoured Personnel Carrier

The M113 Armoured Personnel Carrier series was one of the US Army's veteran vehicles, which saw service in the 1991 war.

Designed by the FMC Corporation, it is a fully tracked, armoured personnel carrier (APC) and first entered service in 1960 to replace the M59, which had been in operation since the early 1950s. The US Army began working on the development of new armoured personnel carriers after World War Two. It was supposed to have better manoeuvrability characteristics than the existing models. It had a new engine to overcome undulating terrain and better armour protection. The military wanted the APC to be deliverable wherever it was needed, even by air.

An innovation in its design was the aluminium alloy armour (the M113 was the first production military vehicle with an aluminium hull). This made it possible to reduce the number of reinforcing

The M113 was used widely by the US Army during Operations *Desert Storm* as an infantry and engineer squad carrier, a medical evacuation carrier, and a maintenance support vehicle. (US DoD)

Above left: Designed by the FMC Corporation, this fully tracked armoured personnel carrier (APC) first entered service in 1961 to replace the M59, which had been in operation since the early 1950s. (US DoD)

Above right: Numerous variants of the M113 were developed. The tracked ambulance allowed medics to access areas of the battlefield that wheeled vehicles would get bogged down in. (US DoD)

Left: Troops sat facing each other and could stow equipment in the centre of the floor area. The rear door could be lowered ramp-style or as a single door with internal handle. (US DoD)

structures and create a more comfortable interior. In its original configuration, the M113 was armed with a 12.7mm machine gun and equipped with a gasoline engine. It was subsequently modernised several times and its armour upgraded. The M113 was used widely by the US Army during Operation *Desert Storm* as an infantry and engineer squad carrier, a medical evacuation carrier, and a maintenance support vehicle. It provided mobile armoured protection for 11 soldiers in full combat gear plus the driver and commander as they moved across the battlefield. Highly reliable, the M113 was a popular platform, but it was vulnerable to a variety of attacks and after the 1991 conflict, a review was carried out into its armour and its future.

Other variants deployed in 1991 included the M163 Vulcan Air Defence System, which was fitted to the hull of an M113 and consisted of a Vulcan gatling gun. The M901 ITV (Improved TOW) was another

The M113 was capable of being airlifted to a forward position by Chinook or down from the United States to a forward staging post by C-5 Galaxy, C17, or C-130. (US DoD).

variant of the M113. Developed in 1985, this M113 variant allowed the crew and weapons system to be shielded from small-arms fire and artillery shrapnel. A periscope allowed the team commander to view the battlefield without exposing himself to danger. The turret launcher could track and acquire targets both during the day and at night. The vehicle could also be transported by air and was amphibious capable. With ten TOW rounds stored on the missile rack, the system could fire two missiles without needing to reload. Tilting the launching device back allows the crew to approach the turret via the carrier's rear roof opening while reloading is carried out behind armour protection. At the end of a revolving arm that lifts the launcher assembly for firing is the missile launcher targeting head. The turret faces down and to the back of the vehicle when it is stowed. First used in battle during Operation *Desert Storm*, the M901 ITV achieved at least 14 kills without suffering any casualties.

M113 Specification	
Model	Armoured Personnel Carrier
Manufacturer	General Motors	General Dynamics Land Systems
Country	United States
Year	1960–present
Engine	Detroit diesel
Fuel	Diesel
Protection	5083 aluminium armour 8–44mm
Top Speed	42mph (67km/h), 4mph in water
Range	300 miles (480km)
Crew Capacity	Two crew, commander, driver, plus 11–15 passengers
Length	15ft
Width	9ft
Height	8ft
Armament	M2 Browning machine gun
Weight	12 tonnes
Service Branch	United States Army

The M901 ITV (Improved TOW) was another variant of the M113. The turret launcher could track and acquire targets both during the day and at night. (US DoD)

Other variants deployed in 1991 included the M163 Vulcan Air Defence System (VADS), which was fitted to the hull of an M113 and consisted of Vulcan gatling gun. (US DoD)

The M163 VADS variant pictured during Operation *Desert Storm* with the gatling gun clearly visible. This was used to shoot down small planes that Coalition commanders feared might be used to spray chemical gas. The driver's head can be seen on the front left of the vehicle and the commander in the turret. (US DoD)

M93A1 Fox – Chemical Reconnaissance System

In the 1990s, the US Army identified a requirement to quickly field a chemical reconnaissance vehicle in response to reports that Saddam Hussein's Army had and was ready to use chemical weapons. In an immediate acquisition programme, the US urgently purchased 48 German-produced vehicles, known as the Fuchs, that met many of the American requirements. These platforms could be totally locked down and sealed from any form of a NBC attack. In addition to the sale, the German government donated an additional 60 vehicles to the US government in support of Operation *Desert Storm*. These vehicles were developed under the project name M93A1 (Fox) and delivered to the US Army and US Marines. The M93A1 Fox is a chemical, biological, radiological and nuclear (CBRN) reconnaissance vehicle developed by both General Dynamics Land Systems (GDLS) and Germany-based Henschel Wehrtechnik. The vehicle can detect, identify, and mark the areas of nuclear and chemical contamination. It can take samples of soil, water, and vegetation to provide accurate information to commanders.

The M93A1 used in the Gulf War was modelled on the German TPz1 Fuchs and has an armoured hull fastened with angled armour panels. This 6x6, all-wheel-drive, armoured vehicle incorporates NBC

Above left: The German NBC vehicles were procured in an Urgent Operational Requirement in readiness for Operation *Desert Storm*, after intelligence concerns that Saddam Hussein's Army had and were ready to use chemical weapons. (DPL)

Above right: The M93A1 Fox is a chemical, biological, radiological and nuclear (CBRN) reconnaissance vehicle developed by both General Dynamics Land Systems and Germany-based Henschel Wehrtechnik. (US DoD)

This 6x6, all-wheel-drive armoured vehicle incorporates NBC detection, warning, and sampling equipment as part of its chemical reconnaissance system. (DPL)

detection, warning, and sampling equipment as part of its chemical-reconnaissance system. Only three crew members are needed to operate the M93A1 due to its automated features. These automated features include a remote sensing chemical agent alarm, the mobile mass spectrometer, chemical agent monitors and an automated chemical agent detector. While an Urgent Operation Requirement prior to the Gulf War, Iraqi forces did not deploy chemical weapons – although the role of the Fox teams in sampling air was critical.

Fox M93A1 / M93A1P1 Specification	
Model	Nuclear Biological Chemical Reconnaissance Vehicle – also Amphibious
Manufacturer	Joint venture between General Dynamics Land Systems (GDLS) and Germany-based Henschel Wehrtechnik	Thyssen-Henschel
Country	United States	Germany
Year	1979–present
Engine	Mercedes-Benz model OM 402A V8 liquid-cooled diesel 320hp
Fuel	Diesel
Protection	Steel armour
Top Speed	65mph (105km/h), 6mph in water
Range	500 miles (800 km)
Crew Capacity	Two crew, commander, driver and ten passengers
Length	22ft
Width	10ft
Height	8ft
Armament	One Rheinmetall MG 3 machine gun, plus two smoke-grenade launchers
Weight	18 tonnes
Service Branch	United States Army	USMC

The Fuchs was designed as an amphibious vehicle. Water propulsion is provided by two four-bladed propellers mounted one each side of the hull at the rear. Maximum water speed is approximately 8 knots. (US DoD)

M548 – Armoured Tracked Cargo Carrier

The US Army deployed the light logistics support vehicle to deliver ammunition to the frontline. The tracked platform was able to drive across wet, soft sand in areas where wheeled vehicles would have struggled. The M548 was very popular and as the crisis in the Gulf loomed, the UK purchased a number of them on an urgent operational requirement. The UK also used the vehicle as an ammunition and stores supply platform. While the cab area was armoured, the relatively lightweight allowed the use of a small engine to power the vehicle, a 6V53 Detroit two stroke, six-cylinder diesel with an Allison TX-100-1 three-speed automatic gearbox. The M548 was one of the more unusual armoured tracked vehicles on the battlefield in 1991. However, its thin steel armour offered limited protection from Iraqi tank attack.

M548 Tracked Armoured Cargo Vehicle Specification	
Model	Tracked Cargo Carrier
Manufacturer	FMC Corp. Oto Melara
Country	United States
Year	1960–present
Engine	Detroit Diesel 6V53, 6-cylinder diesel engine, 204hp
Fuel	Diesel
Protection	Steel cab
Top Speed	38mph (61km/h)
Range	300 miles (482km)
Crew Capacity	Four
Length	19ft
Width	9ft
Height	9ft
Armament	M2 Browning machine gun
Weight	13 tonnes
Service Branch	United States Army	British Army

The M551 Sheridan was a reconnaissance tank, which was deployed in the Gulf War. It was used by the 3rd Battalion (Airborne) 73rd Armoured Cavalry Regiment and was fitted with a thermal sight. During the conflict, the Sheridan force carried out a flank protection role, which saw crews involved in tank-on-tank combat. (US Army)

Chapter 2
United Kingdom

The British Army's tank regiments were put on standby days after Iraq's invasion of Kuwait in 1990. The intervention posed a geo-political oil crisis. If Saddam Hussein gained control of Kuwait and Saudi Arabia, he would have control of more than 20 per cent of world oil reserves and become the world's dominant oil power.

The Challenger main battle tank (MBT) had entered service in 1983. It had been deployed with the British Army on the Rhine and, in 1990, the UK deployed more than 180 to the Middle East. Britain's armoured forces achieved remarkable success in combat, destroying around 300 Iraqi tanks in the Gulf War. A tank crew, from the Royal Scots Dragoon Guards, had the distinction of the longest-range tank-to-tank kill in military history, destroying an Iraqi tank at a range of around 5km (3 miles). In a second example of the tank's capability, a Challenger crew from the 17th/21st Lancers attached to the Queen's Royal Irish Hussars, destroyed an Iraqi T-55 tank at a range of 3,600 metres, using armour-piercing ammunition. After hitting the Iraqi tank, the crew engaged a petrol tanker at a range of 4,700 metres (2.92 miles).

FV403/4 Challenger MBT

The Challenger was the main battle tank of the British Army from 1983 to the mid-1990s. Its deployment to the Gulf War marked its first operational mission. Built by the Royal Ordnance Factory in Leeds, it originated after an Iranian order for an improved version of the Chieftain MBT collapsed in 1979 with the fall of the Shah of Iran in 1979. Two upgraded variants of the Chieftain, known as the Shir 1 and Shir 2, had been produced and remained in the UK. These two prototypes were used as the template for the much-upgraded new tank called the Challenger. The first of the new generation main battle tanks (MBT) entered service with the British Army in 1983.

Above left: The British Army deployed 180 Challenger main battle tanks to the Middle East in 1991. As it waited for the order to move across the start line, the tanks provided flank protection for Coalition forces before they spearheaded the advance into the desert. The 60-ton Challenger was more fuel efficient and achieved a far greater serviceability record than the US Army's M1A1 Abrams. (UK MoD)

Above right: Prior to deployment, the Challenger force spent weeks preparing. The tanks were modified for desert operations by a Royal Electrical and Mechanical Engineers (REME) squadron at the quayside in Al Jubayl, Saudi Arabia. This included additional Chobham armour along the hull sides and Explosive Reactive Armour (ERA) on the nose and front plate. Modifications also included the provision of extra external fuel drums and a smoke generator. (Jack Williams/DPL)

The most advanced aspect of the Challenger design was its integral Chobham armour, which delivered a significant improvement on any other tank in use by Western forces. The tank's cross-country performance was enhanced with hydropneumatics suspension. When it entered service in 1983, the cost of each tank was listed at £2 million. Challenger replaced the Chieftain, a post-war MBT, which was among the most heavily armed tanks in the world when it entered service in the 1960s armed with a 120mm L11 gun.

The main differences between Challenger 1 and its predecessor, the Chieftain, were the engine and the armour. The Challenger engine, which produces 1,200bhp at 2,300rpm, was far more powerful than the Chieftain engine, and its top-secret Chobham armour, which is alleged to protect it from almost all types of anti-tank weapons. At 62 tonnes and with a top speed of 35mph, the tank replaced the Chieftain with an innovative design that was quickly tested in the Gulf. In 1990, the British Army deployed 180

A Challenger operating with a Centurion AVRE during preparations before departing for the Gulf. A small number of the older Centurion platforms were sent to the region as military planners identified that additional armoured engineering units would be needed to head the advance against the Iraqi Army's formidable field fortifications and anti-tank defences. (Jack Williams/DPL)

Above left: Tanks underwent a total engineering check before deployment. The Thermal Observation and Gunnery System (TOGS) fitted to the Challengers proved to be decisive, allowing attacks to be made at night, in poor visibility and through smoke screens. (Magnus Manske)

Above right: A team of drivers flew out to the Middle East to help unload the Challengers from the ship. The tanks were then fitted with their additional armour packages. Additional track, engine and gearbox spares were also shipped out, which the Royal Electrical and Mechanical Engineers would deliver to a logistic hub ready for use. (Jack Williams/DPL)

Challenger tanks to Saudi Arabia on Operation *Granby*, the UK mission within the wider US mission called Operation *Desert Shield*, which was the preparation phase for the 1991 Gulf War.

In the original deployment, the 7th Armoured Brigade included two armoured regiments, the Queen's Royal Irish Hussars and the Royal Scots Dragoon Guards, both equipped with 57 tanks. They were modified for desert operations by the Royal Electrical and Mechanical Engineers (REME) at the quayside in Al Jubail, Saudi Arabia. The modification included additional Chobham armour along the hull sides and explosive reactive armour (ERA) on the nose and front plate. Modifications also included the provision of extra external fuel drums and a smoke generator. There were major concerns about the reliability of the vehicle. In addition, there were serious worries about how a tank designed to perform in a European temperate climate would withstand the rigours of desert warfare.

On 22 November 1990, it was decided to add the 4th Mechanised Brigade to the force, under the umbrella of 1st (UK) Armoured Division. The new brigade had a single Challenger regiment (The 14th/20th King's Hussars) equipped with 43 Challenger 1 tanks and reinforced by a squadron of Life Guards. They were equipped with the Mark 2 version of the tank, which was upgraded by armouring the storage bins for the 120mm charges as well as the additional armour fitted to the Mark 3s.

The main threat to the Challenger was deemed to be the Iraqi Republican Guard's T-72M tank. In action, the Global Positioning System (GPS) and Thermal Observation and Gunnery System (TOGS) fitted to the Challengers proved to be decisive, allowing attacks to be made at night, in poor visibility and through smoke screens. In total, the British Challengers destroyed roughly 300 Iraqi tanks without suffering a single loss in combat. The Challenger, in comparison with the M1A1 Abrams tank, deployed by the US Army, was more fuel efficient and achieved a far greater serviceability record.

The British tanks units of the 1st Armoured Division were assigned to the US VII Corps. With the mission of eliminating the majority of the Iraqi forces, this formation would serve as the Coalition forces' armoured fist. The VII Corps' armour entered Iraq over the Saudi border before entering Kuwait. In the eastern sector of VII Corps' sector, the 1st (UK) Armoured Division, with its Challenger tanks headed the advance. In a series of clashes and battles, the division covered approximately 350km in 97 hours, crushing the Iraqi 52nd Armoured Brigade, 46th Mechanised Brigade, and parts of at least three infantry divisions from the 7th Corps.

In total, 300 Iraqi tanks were either taken prisoner or destroyed, along with dozens of light vehicles, armoured personnel carriers, reconnaissance units, and artillery equipment. The Challenger's stabilised L11A5 120mm rifled gun allowed it to fire on the move. It was very accurate with more than 50 rounds

A Challenger 1 main battle tank of the 7th Armoured Brigade, serving with the 1st Armoured Division, races across the desert towards Kuwait. The British tank units of the 1st Armoured Division were assigned to the US VII Corps – with the mission of eliminating the majority of Iraqi forces. This formation would serve as the Coalition forces' armoured fist. (UK MoD)

carried onboard including high explosive squash head (HESH), armour piercing and smoke. HESH rounds are thin metal shells filled with plastic explosive and a delayed-action fuze at the base of the shell. On impact, the inert material, followed by plastic explosive, is 'squashed' against the surface of the target and spreads out to form a disc or 'pat' of explosive which detonates.

On 26 February 1991, a Challenger, under the command of Captain Tim Purbrick of the 17th/21st Lancers attached to the Queen's Royal Irish Hussars, destroyed an Iraqi T-55 tank at a range of 3,600 metres, using Armour-Piercing Fin-Stabilized Discarding Sabot (APFSDS). Often known as dart ammunition, the make-up of these rounds is highly sensitive – they deliver a type of kinetic energy penetrator using depleted uranium that bores into the hull of modern armour. After hitting the Iraqi tank, his crew engaged a petrol tanker at a range of 4,700 metres again using APFSD rounds.

Challenger 1 Main Battle Tank Specifications	
Model	Challenger
Manufacturer	Royal Ordnance Factory
Country	United Kingdom
Year	1983–2001, subsequently upgraded to Challenger 2
Engine	Perkins CV12 26-litre diesel, 1,200hp
Fuel	Diesel
Protection	Chobham composite ceramic vehicle armour
Top Speed	35mph (60km/h)
Range	280 miles (450km)
Crew Capacity	Four including commander, gunner, loader, driver
Length	38ft
Width	12ft
Height	10ft
Armament	120mm rifled gun	7.62mm machine guns
Weight	62 tonnes
Service Branch	British Army (Royal Tank Regiment & Royal Engineers)

Each Challenger tank had a secret weapon. Although we can't see it, a boiling vessel was fitted inside that allowed the crew to cook its ration packs and make a hot drink. Officially called the 'Vessel Boiling Electric' or 'BV', it was a small container powered by the electrical supply in the tank and could be removed for cleaning and use. (UK MoD)

A Challenger crew pauses at a logistics hub to re-arm its tank. These forward supply bases were manned by the Royal Logistics Corps, which ferried fuel, ammunition and food forward to keep the tanks in action. Recovery and repair teams also deployed to these remote sites to support the crews with maintenance. (UK MoD)

A Challenger crew of the Royal Scots Dragoon Guards await further instructions after securing its objective. Iraqi prisoners can be seen in the background, along with a 432 personnel carrier and the rarely seen M113 tracked ammunition supply vehicle. (UK MoD)

A Challenger escorts a convoy of trucks, which includes a number of Ferret Scout cars. The Challenger's stabilised L11A5 120mm rifled gun allowed it to fire on the move. It was very accurate with more than 50 rounds carried onboard – including a number of 'high explosive squash head' (HESH) rounds. These are thin metal shells filled with plastic explosive and a delayed-action fuze at the base of the shell. On impact, the inert material, followed by plastic explosive, is 'squashed' against the surface of the target and spreads out to form a disc or 'pat' of explosive. The Challenger tanks crews also carried armour piercing and smoke rounds. (UK MoD)

FV4003 Centurion Mk.5 AVRE

As the Gulf War approached, military planners identified that armoured engineering units would be needed to head the advance against the Iraqi Army's formidable field fortifications and anti-tank defences. With that in mind, 12 Centurion tank variants in the Armoured Vehicle Royal Engineers (AVRE) role were deployed to provide the UK armoured force with sufficient engineering support throughout the Gulf War. They were up-armoured with explosive reactive armour (ERA) fitted to the front half of the vehicle in an attempt to defend it against most of the enemy's anti-tank weapons.

The Centurion had entered service in 1945 and was replaced in 1960 with the more modern Chieftain. A number of Chieftain hulls had been converted to the AVRE role and to meet the wide range of tasks, it was decided that the older Centurion AVREs would be deployed. The Centurion platform was fitted with a 165mm L9A1 demolition gun used to clear bunkers. It also had the capability to carry Fascines – big bundles of pipes or branches used to fill up trenches and allow armour to pass and often fitted with a hydraulically operated dozer blade to support a wide range of engineering tasks. The AVRE could haul a 7.5-tonne four-wheel trailer designed to carry a fascine roll, two rolls of Class 60 Trackway, demolition charges, Number 7 Anti-Tank mines, Radiological Dispersal Device (RDD) explosives, and other engineering equipment.

Right: As the Gulf War approached, military planners identified that armoured engineering units would be needed to head the advance against the Iraqi Army's formidable field fortifications and anti-tank defences. With that in mind, 12 Centurion tank variants of the Armoured Vehicle Royal Engineers (AVRE) were deployed to move ahead of the UK armoured force and clear any obstacles. (UK MoD)

Below: The Centurion had entered service in 1945 and was replaced in 1960 with the Chieftain. In this image a Royal Engineers AVRE carried fascines – roles of pipes – which were dropped into holes to allow the tanks to cross. (UK MoD)

The Centurion platform was fitted with a 165mm L9A1 demolition gun used to clear bunkers. It also had the capability to carry fascines – big bundles of pipes or branches – used to fill up trenches and ditches and allow armour to cross. The tank was often fitted with a hydraulically operated dozer blade to support a wide range of engineering tasks. (Jack Williams/DPL)

Above left: In the early 1990s, the Centurion AVRE was still a key part of the Royal Engineers operational equipment, but after 40 years of service, maintenance of the Centurions was a struggle. (UK MoD)

Above right: After the extra amour was fitted, crews trained to operate the 165mm gun. Because of safety regulations, the 165mm on the AVREs had not been fired under-armour (from inside) since the late 1960s. Instead, the crew would load the gun while the tank was in a static position, and then fire via lanyard from outside. (UK MoD)

Another trailer-borne device, which was towed by the AVRE was the 'Giant Viper' mine-clearing system, an upgrade on the World War Two unit called the 'Conger'. The Viper was mounted on a trailer that was towed by the tank. It consisted of a 750ft long, 2⅝in-diameter hose filled with plastic explosives. The Viper would be launched over the tank via a cluster of eight rocket motors, then land in the area that had to be cleared before exploding. The blast would clear a pathway 24ft wide and 600ft long. The device was carried on the back of a unique two-wheel trailer. In the early 1990s, the Centurion AVRE was still a key part of the Royal Engineer's operational equipment, but after 40 years of service, maintenance of the Centurions was a struggle. Crews operating them became known as the 'antiques roadshow' – one of the Centurions that went to the Gulf had taken part in Operation *Motorman* in Northern Ireland almost 20 years earlier.

After the amour was fitted, crews trained to operate the 165mm gun. Because of safety regulations, the 165mm on the AVREs had not been fired under-armour (from inside) since the late 1960s. Instead, the crew would load the gun while the tank was in a static position, and then fire via lanyard from outside. Production of the 165mm ammunition had ended and stocks were low and the AVREs were issued American 165mm ammunition, usually issued to the M728 Combat Engineer Vehicle (CEV).

The US ammunition was 2in longer than the British ammunition, reducing the amount that could be stored inside the tank. Prior to the start of the war, three Centurion AVREs were lost in two separate training incidents, both involving vehicle fires and subsequent detonation of ammunition stored inside the tank. A single AVRE was destroyed in the first incident on 5 February 1991, and two more were lost in the second incident on 6 February 1991.

The first incident is understood to have been caused by petrol fumes that ignited while cooking took place in the vehicle. The second incident was due to accidental ignition of the Giant Viper launch rockets while testing the firing circuits. As a result of the accident, they did not take part in combat operations. However, at the end of the conflict, the Centurions were assigned to a vital task at the Multa Pass, north of Kuwait – the main supply route (MSR) to the northern border with Iraq. It was heavily blocked with wrecks of tanks, trucks and artillery pieces attacked by marauding US A-10 Warthog ground-attack aircraft. Centurions were dispatched to the area along with Chieftain AVREs to clear the burnt-out vehicles and open the road.

Centurion FV4003 Specification	
Model	Centurion AVRE
Manufacturer	Royal Ordnance Factory
Country	United Kingdom
Year	1983–retired from service in 1995
Engine	Rolls-Royce Meteor; five-speed Merrit-Brown Z51R Mk.F gearbox, 650hp
Fuel	Petrol
Protection	Special fit Gulf War – Chobham composite ceramic vehicle armour
Top Speed	21mph (33km/h)
Range	118 miles (190km)
Crew Capacity	Four, including commander, gunner, loader, driver
Length	26ft (hull only), main gun removed
Width	11ft
Height	10ft
Armament	165 AVRE: 165mm L9 Demolition Gun, 105 AVRE: 105mm L7 gun. One coaxial 7.62mm L8A1 (0.3in) machine gun
Weight	57 tonnes
Service Branch	British Army	Royal Engineers

Prior to the start of the war, three Centurion AVREs were lost in two separate training incidents, both involving vehicle fires and subsequent detonation of ammunition stored inside the tank. A single AVRE was destroyed in the first incident on 5 February 1991 and two more were lost in the second incident on 6 February 1991. (UK MoD)

FV4201 Chieftain AVRE

In the first Gulf War, the British Army deployed 14 Chieftain AVREs, from 32 Armoured Regiment Royal Engineers to the Middle East in readiness for operations to eject Saddam's forces from Kuwait. The Chieftain AVREs received extra armour in the form of ERA (which was added to both sides of the crew compartment, adding a total of 1.2 tonnes to the tank. 'Chain mail' was added in the form of a net, which was hung from the 'roof rack' or 'hamper' as protection against shaped-charge ammunition.

The Chieftain MBT was introduced as a replacement for the Centurion, and by the mid-1980s, the Royal Engineers were eager to replace the 40-year-old Centurion AVREs. The Chieftain's replacement, the Challenger I, had started to enter service and as Chieftain tanks became available, they were converted to the AVRE role. The new Chieftain AVRE would be operating alongside the Challenger I. It was required that the vehicle maintained a high level of manoeuvrability and the best power-to-weight ratio possible. To achieve this, the turret was removed saving 12 tonnes. This, however, meant that the 165mm demolition gun was not added to the vehicle, making the Centurion the last armed AVRE used by the Royal Engineers that could deliver firepower. It was fitted with the standard-issue dozer blade, or a modified version of the Centurion 105 AVRE's mine plough and could tow the AVRE trailers containing engineering equipment of two Giant Viper mine-clearing devices.

The turretless hull was fitted with a three-piece superstructure. Known as the roof-rack or hamper, it could carry three PVC 'maxi' pipe fascine rolls or six roles of Class 60 trackway. Six welded legs secured the rack to the hull; the rearmost rack was fixed in place, but the back section of the middle, and the front section of the forward rack, could be raised or lowered hydraulically to drop fascines. It was also decided that the rack be capable of carrying a No. 9 Tank Bridge and other stores. Rollers were attached to the rack to facilitate the loading and unloading of the bridge. It must be stressed that the AVRE could not launch the bridge. It would only carry the No. 9 if it was operating in support of the Chieftain Armoured Vehicle Launcher Bridge (AVLB). In 1991, several of the AVLBs operated by 32 Armoured Regiment Royal Engineers, were fitted with a mine plough.

Above left: In the 1990 Gulf War, the British Army deployed 14 Chieftain AVREs, from 32 Armoured Regiment Royal Engineers to the Middle East in readiness for operations to eject Saddam's forces from Kuwait. The Chieftain AVRE pictured received extra armour in the form of ERA. This variant is fitted with a mine-clearing claw and is carrying a roll of fascines used to fill ditches and is towing a Python mine-clearing system, which shoots a snake of explosives high into the air and on to a minefield, where it explodes, detonating the mines. (UK MoD)

Above right: The Chieftain AVRE pictured is carrying a Fascine – a roll of pipes – during training exercises before the crews deployed to the Gulf. The fascines were discharged from the rack above the driver by remote control and off-loaded into a ditch or obstacle to allow Challenger tanks to cross. The Chieftain AVRE can also tow a Python mine-clearing system, which shoots a snake of explosives high into the air and on to a minefield, where it explodes, detonating the mines.(UK MoD)

The vehicle had a crew of four. This consisted of the commander, driver and two engineers. The driver sat in the standard position at the front of the vehicle. The commander sat in the hull with the two engineers each side of him in very uncomfortable positions due to the low roof.

The AVREs proved very useful in operations in this theatre, serving admirably alongside the Centurion AVREs. Their only real mission, though, was alongside the Centurions clearing the Multa Pass, north of Kuwait. The AVRE's success in the Gulf reinforced an idea from 1989, which called for the conversion of more surplus Chieftain hulls.

Chieftain AVRE Specification	
Model	Chieftain Armoured Vehicle Royal Engineers (AVRE)
Manufacturer	Leyland Motors
Country	United Kingdom
Year	1960s–retired late 1990s
Engine	Leyland L60
Fuel	Petrol	multi-fuel
Protection	Special fit Gulf War, Chobham composite ceramic vehicle armour
Top Speed	25mph (40km/h)
Range	310 miles (500km)
Crew Capacity	Four, including commander, gunner, loader, driver
Length	25ft (hull only), main gun removed
Width	12ft
Height	10ft
Armament	Main gun removed
Weight	43 tonnes. (Main gun reduced weight by 12 tonnes)
Service Branch	British Army	Royal Engineers

Above left: In 1991, several Chieftain AVLBs, again operated by 32 Armoured Regiment Royal Engineers, were deployed, fitted with the Number 8 bridge capable of spanning a gap of 78 metres. The AVLBs could also carry a mine-clearing claw at the front. (UK MoD)

Above right: The Chieftain AVRE's carried out extensive training before deploying. They carried fascines, which could be used to fill ditches and enable other vehicles to cross them as well as a wide range of engineer tasks. (Jack Williams/DPL)

FV107 Combat Vehicle Reconnaissance (Tracked)

The introduction of the Combat Vehicle Reconnaissance (Tracked) (CVR(T)) reconnaissance, also known as the FV107 and 'support vehicles' in the 1970s introduced a new family of vehicles, all of which were based on the same basic design and were to see action in the Gulf War. The Scimitar armed reconnaissance light tank, the Samaritan armoured ambulance, the Sultan command and control vehicle, the Striker anti-tank guided missile vehicle, Samson armoured recovery vehicle and Spartan personnel carrier delivered special capability. Developed by Alvis the design initially incorporated a petrol engine, which was replaced with a diesel unit during an upgrade.

FV107 Scimitar

A fast highly effective platform. Scimitar units were often deployed to provide support to infantry troops and had the ability as an unofficial battle taxi with soldiers sat on the chassis. It was issued to Royal Armoured Corps regiments in the reconnaissance role. Each regiment originally had a close reconnaissance squadron of five troops, each containing eight FV107 Scimitars. Each Main Battle Tank Regiment also employed eight Scimitars in the close reconnaissance role. During the 1991 Gulf War, the divisional reconnaissance regiment attached to the 1st Armoured Division was the 16th/5th The Queen's Royal Lancers, with 36 Scimitars, 16 Strikers, 12 Spartans, nine Sultans and four Samaritans, as well as 'A' Squadron 1st Queen's Dragoon Guards with 16 Scorpions, four Spartans, two Sultans, one Samaritan and one Samson. During one engagement, a troop of Scimitars from the Dragoon Guards engaged and destroyed several Iraqi T-62s penetrating their armour with sabot rounds.

FV101 Scorpion

A light tank and armoured reconnaissance vehicle, the Scorpion was fitted with the heavier 76mm gun. Like the Scimitar, it was fast and highly capable. During the Gulf War, the platform was deployed with the 16th/5th Queen's Royal Lancers. The Scorpion served from 1973 and was removed from service in 1994. More than 3,000 were built and the low velocity 76mm L23A1 cannon, which was capable of firing high-explosive, HESH (High Explosive Squash Head). It is a type of explosive ammunition that is effective against buildings and is also used against tank armour. The Scorpion could also fire smoke and canister rounds were mounted on the Scorpion. There was room to store 40 or 42 rounds. In addition, the Scorpion had two multi-barrelled smoke grenade dischargers, one on each side of the turret, and a 7.62mm coaxial L7 General Purpose Machine Gun (GPMG) with 3,000 rounds carried, were also installed.

The Scorpion, light armoured reconnaissance vehicle, was fitted with the heavier 76mm gun. Like the Scimitar, it was fast and highly capable. During the Gulf War, the platform was deployed with the 16th/5th Queen's Royal Lancers. The Scorpion served from 1973 and was removed from service in 1994. (UK MoD)

FV104 Samaritan

The FV104 Samaritan was the armoured ambulance used by the British Army in the Gulf War. Manned by soldiers from the Royal Army Medical Corps, it provided protected mobility to evacuate wounded soldiers from the battlefield. Inside the vehicle, space was tight with four stretchers and a narrow passageway for medics to treat patients. It had the capability to ferry six casualties from the frontline to a regimental medical station. As part of their combat service support, almost all armoured units were supported by Samaritan ambulance units.

FV105 Sultan

The FV105 Sultan was a British command-and-control vehicle based on the CVR(T) platform. It has a higher roof than the armoured personnel carrier (Spartan) variants, providing a more comfortable 'office space' inside. Sultan entered service in 1978 and served with the 1st Armoured Division in the Gulf War giving commanders a planning office on the frontline. The Sultan was one of many vehicles (7,000 in all) that the UK military shipped to the Gulf in readiness for operations to eject Iraqi forces from Kuwait.

Above left: A fast, highly effective platform, Scimitar units were often deployed to provide support to infantry troops and had the ability to be an unofficial battle taxi with soldiers sat on the chassis. It was issued to Royal Armoured Corps armoured regiments in the reconnaissance role. (UK MoD)

Above right: The FV103 Spartan shared a similar appearance to the FV102 Striker. The Spartan could accommodate seven people, divided into two crew members and five passengers, or three crew members and four passengers. It had one 7.62mm L37A1 machine gun and four smoke dischargers that could be mounted on each side. (DPL)

FV102 Striker

The FV102 Striker was the anti-tank guided missile carrier in the CVR(T) family. The British Army developed the Striker to launch the Swingfire missile. Delivered in 1975, the first production vehicles were employed by the Royal Artillery anti-tank guided missile batteries in the British Army. On 24 March 2003, a Striker destroyed an Iraqi T-55 tank with an anti-tank missile. The FV102 Striker was withdrawn from British Army service as the Swingfire missile was replaced by the Javelin missile in mid-2005.

FV106 Samson

The main role of this vehicle was to recover the CVR(T) family of vehicles, but it could also recover other light tracked vehicles such as the older 430 series. The Samson was conceived in the early 1970s with the final design entering production in 1978. The hull is an all-welded aluminium construction. It usually carries a crew of three, operating a 3.5 tonne capstan winch that can also be utilised in a lifting

Left: A Scimitar on a live firing mission prior to the start of the Gulf War in February 1991. The reconnaissance vehicle was popular with crews for its speed and reliability. Most were withdrawn from UK service in 2023. (Jack Williams/DPL)

Below: The Scimitar CVRT delivered a fast, reliable, armoured reconnaissance capability to the 1st Armoured Division of the UK force in the Gulf during Operation *Granby*. The Scimitar was the 'armoured sports car' of the battlefield. It had a crew of three, a Rarden 30mm cannon and was initially fitted with a 4.2-litre cylinder Jaguar engine. (Bob Morrison/DPL)

configuration. It carries suitable equipment to enable a 4:1 mechanical advantage with 228m of winch rope. This winch is capable of recovering up to 12 tonnes of vehicle. A manually operated earth anchor was situated at the rear to anchor the vehicle while operations were carried out.

FV103 – Spartan

The British Army's FV103 Spartan was the tracked armoured personnel carrier of the CVR(T) family. In 1978, the vehicle was deployed by the British military. With the exception of the Striker's missile launcher, the Spartan shares a similar appearance with the FV102 Striker. The Spartan can accommodate seven people, divided into two crew members and five passengers or three crew members and four passengers. It has one 7.62mm L37A1 machine gun and four smoke dischargers that can be mounted on each side. The Spartan was deployed in the Gulf War.

Combat Vehicle Reconnaissance (Tracked) Specifications	
Model	Scimitar, Scorpion, Striker, Spartan, Samaritan, Sultan, Samson
Manufacturer	Alvis | BAE Systems
Country	United Kingdom
Year	1970s–retired 2022
Engine	Jaguar J60 4.2-litre petrol | later replaced with Cummins BTA 5.9-litre diesel
Fuel	Petrol | diesel
Protection	Aluminium alloy armour
Top Speed	50mph (80km/h)
Range	300 miles (482km)
Crew Capacity	Three to seven depending on variant
Length	15ft
Width	7ft
Height	7ft
Armament	30mm Rarden cannon on Scimitar | 76mm gun on Scorpion
Weight	8 tonnes (main gun reduced weight by 12 tonnes)
Service Branch	British Army | Royal Engineers

Scimitar variants pictured in the desert during pre-deployment training. As well as the Scimitar, the family of vehicles included the Samaritan, Striker, Spartan and Samson. (Jack Williams/DPL)

FV432 – Armoured Personnel Carrier

The British Army's FV430 series of armoured combat vehicles entered service in the 1970s – with the iconic 432 becoming the workhorse of armoured infantry operations. In 1991, the 432 was sent to the Gulf, Operation *Granby*, and was a key tracked mobility platform for the 1st Armoured Division. It was seen as a multi-functional, reliable vehicle, although unlike many other platforms, it never gained recognition with a name and was simply known as the 432.

It was due to be phased out as the Warrior entered service, but its robust capability ensured it survived into the Gulf War and beyond. Produced by GKN Sankey, more than 3,000 vehicles were delivered to the British Army. This powerful APC was fitted with a Rolls-Royce water-cooled petrol engine, giving the vehicle a top speed of 32mph on the road. It was an all-steel construction; the chassis was a conventional tracked design with the engine at the front and the driving position to the right. Directly behind the

Above left: In 1991, the 432 was sent to the Gulf, to take part in Operation *Granby*, and was a key tracked mobility platform for the 1st Armoured Division. More than 20 variants of the 432 ambulance variant were deployed to the Middle East. The rear compartment could carry four stretcher patients or as many as ten walking wounded. (UK MoD)

Above right: An FV432 armoured personnel carrier of the 7th Brigade Royal Scots, 1st United Kingdom Armoured Division, crosses into Kuwait from southern Iraq during Operation *Desert Storm*. The 432 was deployed as a command platform, as well as a personnel carrier, ambulance and recovery platform. (UK MoD)

Above left: An ambulance 432 and a Samaritan (CVRT family) at a forward operating base in the desert during the Gulf War. This powerful APC was fitted with a Rolls-Royce water-cooled petrol engine, giving the vehicle a top speed of 32mph on the road. (UK MoD)

Above right: A 432s recovery variant at a desert location. The heavy winch can be seen on the side of the vehicle. These tracked carriers followed the main advance force and were ready to repair and provide assistance in a military roadside recovery role. (UK MoD)

driver's position is the vehicle commander's hatch. There is a large round opening in the passenger compartment roof, which has a split hatch, and a side-hinged door in the rear for loading and unloading. As in many designs of its era, there are no firing ports for the troops carried – British Army doctrine has always been to dismount from vehicles to fight, unlike Russian infantry fighting vehicles that largely incorporate weapon ports.

Above left: The rear troop-carrying compartment of the 432. The seats could be raised and stretchers fitted, or a table fitted and the space used for a command planning team. Further configurations allow the 432 to operate as a recovery platform and as an observation post for gunner teams. (UK MoD)

Above right: A 432 crew pass a burning Iraq BRDM-2 as the battle comes to a close. The exhaust chamber can clearly be seen on the side of the vehicle and again it appears to have stores and supplies above. (UK MoD)

A 432 in what appears to be the 'command mode' and bearing US Army-style 'recon' insignis, suggesting it was part of the forward headquarters operating alongside US forces. Crews often stacked rations and water on top of the vehicle. The inverted 'V' indicated it was part of the Coalition force. (UK MoD)

The passenger compartment has five seats on each side – these fold up to provide a flat cargo space. The 432 could deliver troops, it had capacity for ten, but often more, and would deliver them as close to a battle as possible.

Its only armament was a single 7.62mm General Purpose Machine Gun (GPMG) and smoke dischargers fitted to the front armour.

The family of vehicles included ambulance variants as well as variants used by the Royal Engineers in mine clearing and the Royal Artillery as battery command posts and to carry Cyberline mortar-locating radar teams. The FV432 was a flexible, robust vehicle that could easily be converted to a command role, a cargo carrier, a communications platform, a recovery vehicle, and as an anti-tank platform. In 1990, the 432 and its family of variants were among the first to be ferried to the Gulf.

FV 432 Tracked Armoured Personnel Carrier Specification	
Model	Armoured Personnel Carrier – Variants were modified for medical, command and communications
Manufacturer	GKN Sankey
Country	United Kingdom
Year	1960s–retired 2023
Engine	Rolls-Royce K60 multi-fuel 240hp
Fuel	Multi-fuel
Protection	12.7mm steel hull – ad hoc armour fitted on operations
Top Speed	32mph (51km/h)
Range	360 miles (580km)
Crew Capacity	Crew of two plus ten passengers
Length	17ft (hull only), main gun removed
Width	8ft
Height	8ft
Armament	7.62mm general-purpose machine gun
Weight	15 tonnes
Service Branch	British Army

FV510 – Warrior (Tracked Armoured Vehicle)

The Warrior FV510 is the mainstay of the British Army's armoured infantry force, a solid and capable vehicle that has delivered reliability on operations since entering service. The Warrior tracked vehicle family is a series of British armoured vehicles, originally developed to replace the FV430 series of armoured vehicles. The Warrior started life as the MCV-80 (Mechanised Combat Vehicle for the 1980s).

One of the requirements of the new vehicle was a top speed able to keep up with the projected new main battle tank, which was eventually named as the Challenger. The project started in 1972 and GKN Defence won the production contract. The first unit to receive the Warrior was the 1st Battalion Grenadier Guards in Germany, followed by the 1st Battalion of the Staffordshire Regiment, between 1987 and 1988. This armoured personnel carrier was quickly integrated into the British Army in a mechanised infantry role and was one of the UK government's procurement success stories. The project produced a family of Warrior variants, including a command vehicle, repair and recovery

Warriors sprayed in desert colours and waiting to be loaded aboard a ship for transit to the Middle East in 1990, prior to the 1991 Gulf War. The Warrior became the workhorse of the British Army's armoured infantry force in the 1991 Gulf War. (UK MoD)

The Warrior delivered speed, reliability and was able to operate in most terrains. The driver kept his hatch open in the desert, when not engaged with the enemy, to generate some cool air amid the baking heat. (UK MoD)

The Warrior family of seven variants of armoured vehicles, which entered service in 1988, had been highly successful for armoured infantry battlegroups. The vehicle provided excellent mobility, lethality and survivability for the infantry and enabled key elements from the Royal Artillery and Royal Electrical and Mechanical Engineers to operate effectively within the battle group. (UK MoD)

Warriors on the so-called 'highway of death' after Coalition forces ambushed Iraqi forces in February 1991. A Warrior's crew included the commander and gunner in the turret, and the driver, located in the front hull. Up to seven soldiers could be carried, seated in the rear hull. (UK MoD)

A Warrior crew from the the 1st Battalion Grenadier Guards stop to assist any Iraqi wounded soldiers on the main road out of Kuwait north towards the Iraq border. This armoured personnel carrier was quickly integrated into the British Army in a mechanised infantry role and was one of the UK government's procurement success stories. (UK MoD)

Warrior crews flew British flags from their vehicles as an indicator to US warplanes that they were 'friendly forces'. There were several incidents in which Coalition vehicles were mistakenly attacked by US aircraft. The aim of flying the flag was to give a clear indicator to low flying aircraft that the Warriors were part of the Coalition force. (UK MoD)

Vehicle, Observation Post Vehicle (OPV) and ad-hoc Ambulance – although this was not a structured role. During the 1991 Gulf War, Warrior regiments were deployed with the 7th and 4th Armoured Brigades ferrying troops to the frontline.

A Warrior's crew included the commander and gunner in the turret, and the driver, who is located in the front hull. Up to seven soldiers can sit in the rear hull compartment facing one another. The rear of the hull has an electric ram-powered door that allows passengers to enter. For a 48-hour warfare day in nuclear, biological, and chemical environments, seven fully outfitted soldiers, supplies and weapons—including many anti-tank weapons—can be carried in Warrior section vehicles. A four-speed automated gearbox propels the Perkins-Rolls-Royce V8 Condor engine that powers the Warrior. It can travel at a speed of 46mph (74km/h) on the road. Over the roughest terrain, the Warrior's performance and speed allow it to maintain a competitive edge over a Challenger 2 main battle tank.

The vehicle has a two-man GKN Sankey turret that is equipped with a L94A1 EX-34 7.62mm Hughes Helicopters coaxial chain gun and a non-stabilised L21A1 30mm Rarden cannon that can destroy some APCs at a maximum range of 1,500m (1,600yd). It has two four-defensive grenade launcher clusters installed, which are typically employed in conjunction with Visual and Infrared Screening Smoke, or VIRSS.

Variants of the Warrior included the following:

FV512 – Mechanised Combat Repair Vehicle
Operated by REME detachments in Armoured Infantry battalions. It is equipped with a 6.5-tonne crane plus power tools and is able to tow a trailer carrying two Warrior power packs or one Challenger power pack. In total, 105 of these were produced.

FV513 – Mechanised Recovery Vehicle (Repair)
Also operated by REME detachments in armoured infantry battalions. It is equipped with a 20-tonne winch and 6.5-tonne crane plus power tools and (like the FV512) is able to tow a trailer carrying two Warrior power packs or one Challenger power pack. In total, 39 of these were produced.

FV 514 – Mechanised Artillery Observation Vehicle
This is operated by the Royal Artillery as an Artillery Observation Post Vehicle (OPV) and is fitted with mast-mounted Man-packable Surveillance and Target Acquisition Radar (MSTAR) and Position and Azimuth Determining System (PADS), with image-intensifying and infra-red equipment. The only armament is the 7.62mm machine gun, as the 30mm Rarden cannon is replaced by a dummy weapon. This allows space for the targeting and surveillance equipment while retaining largely the same outward appearance of a standard Warrior in order to avoid becoming a priority target. In total, 52 of these were produced.

Warriors have seen action in Operation *Granby*. Unfortunately, two American Fairchild Republic A-10 Thunderbolt II ground-attack aircraft accidentally discharged two AGM-65 Maverick missiles, destroying two Warriors and killing nine men in a friendly fire incident. The Royal Scots Dragoon Guards and Queen's Royal Irish Hussars in Challenger I and 1 Stafford in Warrior formed the 7th Armoured Brigade. With 1st Battalion Royal Scots and 3rd Battalion Royal Regiment of Fusiliers in Warrior, together with 14th/20th King's Hussars in their Challengers, the 4th Armoured Brigade was predominantly composed of infantry. Personnel from the Grenadier Guards would reinforce these two brigades. All variations together accounted for more than 250 Warriors sent to the Middle East.

Warrior – Tracked Armoured Vehicle Specification	
Model	Warrior FV. 430 (MCV-80)
Manufacturer	GKN Sankey
Country	UK
Year	1987–present
Engine	Perkins V-8 Condor Diesel 550hp
Diesel	Diesel
Protection	Aluminium and appliqué
Top Speed	46mph (74km/h)
Range	410 miles (659km)
Crew Capacity	Crew of three, plus maximum 10 personnel
Length	20ft
Width	10ft
Height	9ft
Armament	30mm L21A1 Rarden cannon
Weight	25 tonnes
Service Branch	British Army

Ferret – Armoured Car (Ferret Scout Car)

The British armoured fighting vehicle known as the Ferret was created as a reconnaissance platform and was deployed in the 1991 Gulf War, despite being 40 years old at the time of mobilisation. The Ferret was used in a number of roles including by Royal Artillery air defence teams. The vehicles were manufactured by Daimler and first introduced in the 1950s. Space inside was cramped and the driver's steering wheel was a large, angled yoke, which often took drivers a while to become familiar with.

Above left: The British armoured fighting vehicle known as the Ferret armoured fighting vehicle was created as a reconnaissance platform and was deployed in the 1991 Gulf War, despite being 40 years old at the time of mobilisation. (UK MoD)

Above right: Ferret Scout cars can be seen to the right of the picture and in the centre providing armed escort for British supply convoys during the 1991 Gulf War. This was the last operation for the two-man armoured vehicle. (UK MoD)

The Ferret suspension, like the previous Daimler Scout car, was made up of single coil springs and pairs of transverse links. The wheels were driven by Tracta constant – velocity joints drove the wheels of the Ferret. However, the six-cylinder, 4.26-litre water-cooled Rolls-Royce B.60 petrol engine on the Ferret was made possible by epicyclic reduction gears, which reduced gearbox torque loads. It was very powerful and fast. With the exception of six forward-firing grenade launchers fitted to the hull over the front wheels (which are typically fitted with smoke grenades), the basic vehicle was open-topped and unarmed. Crew quickly adopted a .303 Bren light machine gun and, in an upgrade, a mounted .30mm Browning machine gun was fixed in a permanent turret. When the Irish Hussars deployed to Saudi Arabia as part of the 7th Armoured Brigade in preparation for Operation *Desert Storm*, the vehicle went with them. In October 1990, the Ferret force was discharged from a 'ship taken up from trade' in the port of Al Jubail. The vehicles quickly deployed in the desert, but after operations in Lebanon, Malaya, Aden and Northern Ireland, the Gulf War was the final mission for the Ferret.

Ferret – Armoured Reconnaissance Car Specification	
Model	Ferret (FV 701)
Manufacturer	Daimler (UK)
Country	UK
Year	1952–91
Engine	Rolls-Royce B60 Inlet over Exhaust 16 petrol
Diesel	Petrol
Protection	Aluminium and appliqué
Top Speed	58mph (93km/h)
Range	190 miles (305km)
Crew Capacity	Two
Length	12ft
Width	6ft
Height	6ft
Armament	7.62mm NATO standard GPMG – 30 M1919 Browning machine gun
Weight	3.7 tonnes
Service Branch	British Army

TPz Fuchs

Concern that Saddam Hussein would use chemical weapons against coalition forces in 1990 resulted in the British Army seeking additional protection. The German government gave the UK a total of 11 German Army Fuchs vehicles to support ground reconnaissance and electronic warfare in the First Gulf War of February 1991. The six-wheeled, armoured vehicles offered total protection in a nuclear, biological and chemical environment and were vital to UK forces amid claims that Iraqi forces would deploy Sarin gas. Developed by Germany's Daimler-Benz, Rheinmetall MAN Military Vehicles (RMMV) the vehicle had been ordered for the Bundeswehr (West Germany Army). As well as its off-road capability, the Fuchs is fully amphibious with a maximum water speed of 10 knots.

As well as its primary NBC role, the platform can also be used for electronic warfare, medical evacuation, a mortar team carrier and for bomb disposal tasks. The Fuchs' hull is made entirely of welded armoured steel. The vehicle commander is seated to the right of the driver, who sits in the front, on the

British Fuchs NBC vehicles are washed down during an exercise to prepare crews to decontaminate their trucks if they faced a chemical attack. The Fuchs were procured on an Urgent Operational Deployment from Germany after fears that Saddam Hussein would use chemical weapons against Coalition forces. A total of 11 Fuchs vehicles, tasked with NBC, ground reconnaissance and electronic warfare were deployed. (UK MoD)

Left: During Operation *Granby*, the Fuchs vehicles played a key role in testing and evaluating air samples. The remote-controlled systems allowed operators inside the Fuchs to view the ground though a gas-tight window and camera. Soldiers wore sealed suits to protect their hands when they used hand-held systems to take air samples. (UK MoD)

Below: A robotic series of arms could be used to recover samples of sand for testing. This hi-tech equipment included cameras to monitor the sampling. Specialist crews use these remote-controlled tools to recover samples of soil and rocks via a gas-tight porthole in the rear door. (UK MoD)

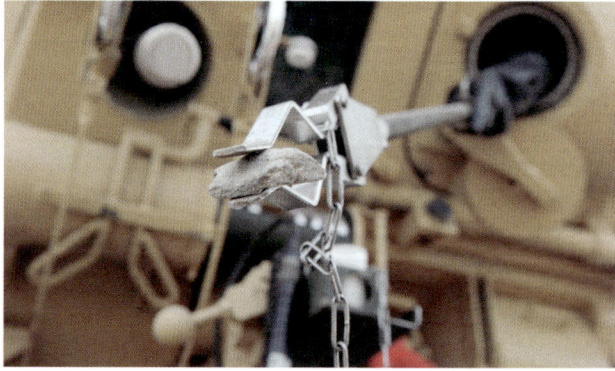

left. The commander and driver each have their own door. There are metal shutters on the windscreen and door windows that can be closed to seal the vehicle. Periscopes installed in the vehicle's roof, forward of the driver's hatch, provide views outside the cabin. There is a circular roof hatch for the commander. During Operation *Granby*, the Fuchs vehicles played a key role in testing and evaluating air samples. After the war, the UK formed a joint NBC squadron of RAF and Royal Tank Regiment personnel who provide specialist support across British armed forces.

FUCHS – Armoured NBC Reconnaissance Vehicle Specification	
Model	TPz Fuchs – Nuclear, Chemical, Biological, Reconnaissance
Manufacturer	Daimler Benz
Country	Germany
Year	1979–present
Engine	Mercedes Benz Model OM 402 A V8 liquid-cooled diesel engine
Diesel	Diesel
Protection	Steel armour
Top Speed	65mph (105km/h)
Range	500 miles (804km)
Crew Capacity	Crew of two, plus ten personnel
Length	22ft
Width	10ft
Height	8ft
Armament	MG3 Rheinmetall machine gun
Weight	20 tonnes
Service Branch	British Army

British Fuchs NBC vehicles flying the Union Jack. Many units flew flags in order to alert Coalition fighter aircraft that they were friendly forces. (UK MoD)

Chapter 3

France

France was quick to join the multi-national Coalition in the Middle East, deploying 18,000 soldiers, including elements of the French Foreign Legion. From the outset, the Paris administration showed no hesitation in joining the military alliance against Saddam Hussein. Within days of the Iraq invasion of Kuwait, the late President Francois Mitterrand insisted that France would not tolerate Iraqi aggression and that France was ready to fight alongside its allies – although Mitterrand also demanded that every diplomatic means possible be employed to resolve the crisis.

The spearhead of the nation's force, known as the Daguet Division, included a regiment of AMX-30 tanks. It was fast, modern and highly regarded for its fire-power accuracy. The French force operated on the left flank of the US XVIII Airborne Corps and was tasked with capturing the Al Salman Air Base – a Kuwait air base, which the Iraqis had captured. The French Foreign Legion deployed with Véhicule de L'Avant Blindé (VAB) armoured personnel carrier,s which they used to drive to their objectives. This chemical-warfare-protected wheeled vehicle performed well in the desert and was upgraded after the conflict.

AMX-30 Main Battle Tank

The AMX-30 is a main battle tank developed by GIAT Industries in the 1960s and was the spearhead force of France's Task Force deployed to the Gulf War in 1991. Paris sent a total of 46 AMX-30s to support its operation within the Coalition. It was ordered as a replacement for the French Army's M-47s and was equipped with an 105mm gun as primary armament. Its auxiliary armament consists of a 20mm cannon and a 7.62mm machine gun. It is powered by a 720/680hp diesel engine, which allows for a top speed of 40mph on surface roads. The AMX-30 also features NBC protection and reached its provisional readiness, known as Initial Operating Capability (IOC) in 1966 with the French Army. The initial production version of the AMX-30B weighed 36 tonnes and had a crew of four – driver, gunner, loader and commander.

The AMX-30 was developed by GIAT Industries in the 1960s and was the spearhead force of France's Task Force deployed to the Gulf War in 1991. Paris sent a total of 44 AMX-30s to support its operation within the Coalition. The vehicle was fast, reliable and carried a crew of four. (French Armed Forces)

Prior to deployment, the AMX-30 tank force spent weeks exercising in France. The tank was the lightest tank within NATO, with a weight similar to the Soviet T-54/55. The front of the hull was sloped in order to deflect attacks and maintain a low profile on radar. (French Armed Forces).

In 1991, the French Army was among the first to support the Arab Coalition. Instead of the 52 tanks that were typically present in a unit, an experimental new regimental organisational structure was implemented, which consisted of three squadrons of 13 tanks, a command tank, and six reserve vehicles. (French Armed Forces).

The French Army accepted 1,355 AMX-30s into service. The vehicle underwent numerous upgrades, which included a new stabilised gun system in the early 1970s, and in 1979, a major upgrade was introduced under the designation of AMX-30B2. (French Armed Forces)

The AMX-30 was the lightest NATO tank, with a weight similar to the Soviet T-54/55. The front of the hull was sloped in order to make deflect attacks and maintain a low profile. The tank also had two banks of smoke grenade launchers on each side of the vehicle and the turret was selected on the earlier AMX-30 prototype designs – although its shape was modified especially at the back. The 105mm gun could elevate to more than 20 degrees and was loaded manually with a storage capability for 47 rounds of ammunition.

The secondary armament was a coaxial mounted 12.7mm machine gun, which was later upgraded to the CN 20 F2 20mm automatic cannon. This was introduced for use against soft vehicles (lightly armoured) and low-flying targets. A searchlight was mounted at the front of the turret that could operate in both white light and the infra-red (IR) mode. The final production vehicle retained many of the properties of the prototype, although the engine was replaced with a Hispano-Suiza HS 110 680hp diesel paired with the 5SD-200D mechanical gearbox allowing the tank to reach a speed of 40mph on surface roads. The engine was designed in a 'power pack' unit, which allowed mechanics to remove and replace the entire engine unit in 45 minutes.

Mass production commenced in 1966 and more than 3,500 AMX-30s and its variants were built. The French Army accepted 1,355 in service. It underwent numerous upgrades, which included a new stabilised gun system in the early 1970s, and in 1979, a major upgrade was introduced under the designation of AMX-30B2. In the early 1980s, a new gearbox was fitted and further enhancements made to the engine. Variants to the main battle tank included a surface-to-air missile launcher, the AMX-30D armoured recovery vehicle, the AMX-30R anti-aircraft gun system, a bridge-layer, and the AMX-30T tactical nuclear missile launcher. The AMX-30T was rarely seen and remained as part of France's nuclear deterrent.

Instead of the 52 tanks that were typically present in a unit, an experimental new regimental organisational structure was implemented for operations in the Gulf, which consisted of three squadrons of 13 tanks, a command tank, and six reserve vehicles. In addition, six older AMX-30Bs were put into service, renamed the AMX 30 Demin, and deployed in a mine-clearing role. France's 6e Division Légère Blindée (6th Light Armoured Division) was deployed as part of the main force in Operation *Daguet*, the French name within Operation *Desert Storm*, and later became known as the 'Division Daguet'.

The 4e Regiment de Dragons (4th Dragoon Regiment), was dispatched with 44 AMX-30B2s and tasked to protect the left flank of the American XVIII Airborne Corps. The Daguet Division was stationed to the west of the Coalition force to protect it and engage any Iraqi armoured units. (French Armed Forces).

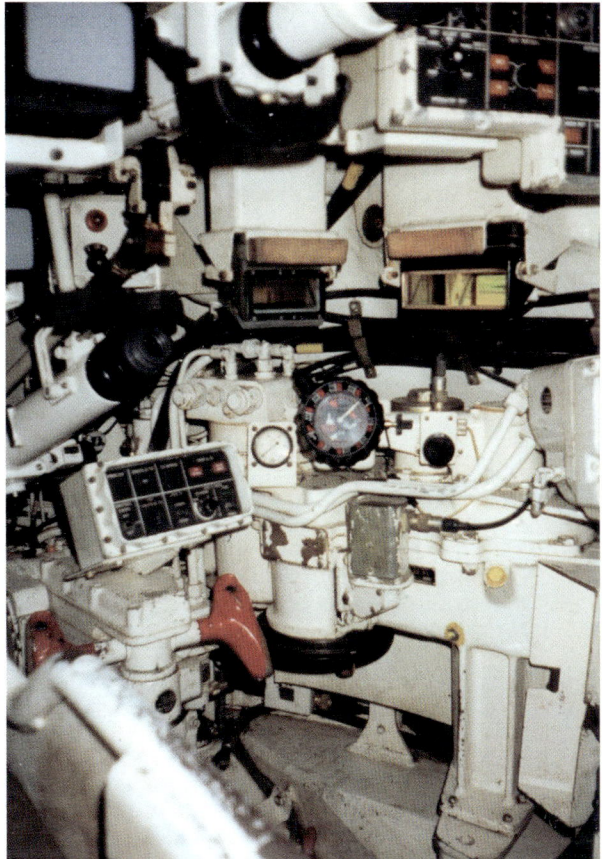

Right: Inside the AMX-30 there was little space for the four-strong crew to direct, load and fire the 105mm Module F1 gun. Produced by GIAT, the tank had a top speed of 40mph and an endurance of 370 miles. (French Armed Forces)

Below: The AMX-30D armoured recovery vehicle was deployed with the main battle tanks. Variants of the main battle tank included a surface-to-air missile launcher, the AMX-30R anti-aircraft gun system, a bridge-layer, and the AMX-30T tactical nuclear missile launcher. (French Armed Forces)

The 4e Régiment de Dragons (4th Dragoon Regiment) was dispatched with 44 AMX-30B2s and tasked to protect the left flank of the American XVIII Airborne Corps, the Daguet Division was stationed to the west of the Coalition force to protect the force and engage any Iraqi armoured units. On 24 February 1991, French soldiers launched their ground offensive, attacking 'Objective Rochambeau' in which French tanks supported the French Foreign Legion to secure their first objective, which was held by Iraq's 45th Infantry Division unit. An aviation strike crippled the Iraqi armour allowing the 4e Régiment de Dragoons to attack with decisive success. The French tank commanders were aware of the capability of the Iraqi tanks and their heavier armour.

Captain Allavena, a commander with the 4th Dragoon armoured regiment said: 'We knew we would be facing T-55s and at 1,500 metres they are a threat to us, so we flanked them and hit them from the side. We discovered many were dug in and we blocked their escape.'

The AMX-30B2s were soon in action again moving on Objective 'Chambord'. With the help of the USAF A-10s, they were able to destroy ten tanks, three BMPs, 15 trucks, and five mortars in addition to taking dozens of prisoners. The ultimate goal was the As-Salman Air Base, also known as Objective 'White', which was captured in a multi-faceted assault led by the AMX-30B2s of the Dragoons, which attacked from the south. The AMX-30s fired 270 rounds from their main guns in all.

AMX-30B Main Battle Tank Specification	
Model	AMX-30B Main Battle Tank – later upgraded to AMX-30 B2
Manufacturer	GIAT
Country	France
Year	1960s–retired 2023
Engine	Hispano-Suiza HS-110 multi-fuel 680hp
Fuel	Multi-fuel
Protection	Steel hull, 3 in
Top Speed	40mph (64km/h)
Range	370 miles (595km)
Crew Capacity	Four
Length	31ft
Width	10ft
Height	8ft
Armament	105mm module F1 tank gun
Weight	36 tonnes
Service Branch	French Army

AMX-10RC Armoured Car

The AMX-10RC armoured reconnaissance vehicle arrived in the Persian Gulf in late 1990 and prepared to operate ahead of the AMX 30 tanks to provide intelligence on enemy forces. A total of 90 AMCX-10RCs supported the French operation and despite the soft sand, the vehicle's 6x6-wheeled configuration, allowed it to traverse all types of terrain more easily than most tracked MBTs. It had a top speed of around 35mph on surfaced roads and a range of approximately 300 miles.

Developed by Nexter Systems, it entered service in 1981 and many describe the platform as a 'tank destroyer on wheels'. The AMX-10 RC is typically utilised for fire support in operations where the vehicle

Above: A group of AMX-10RCs operating in the desert during the 1991 war. The French deployed 90 variants of the AMX-10RC in the Gulf War. Despite the desert sand, the vehicle's 6x6 wheeled configuration allowed it to traverse all types of terrain more easily than most tracked MBTs. It had a top speed of around 50mph on surfaced roads and a range of approximately 300 miles. (French Armed Forces)

Right: Upgrades to the vehicles included a new battlefield management system called Finders C2R. A further enhancement improved traction on uneven ground and a central tyre inflation mechanism allows the driver to set pressure in respect of driving conditions. (French Armed Forces)

supports troops on the ground with sustained fire or engages deliberate targets, as well as mounting reconnaissance missions.

The AMX-10 RC started development in 1970 with prototypes being tested by 1976. The first production vehicle was delivered in 1981 to the 2nd Regiment de Hussars in Sourdun. The vehicle's GIAT 105mm cannon is mounted in a turret made of welded aluminium. The driver is seated at the front of the hull, while three crew members are housed behind in the turret. For gun targeting, a fire-control system, known as COTAC, is installed to assist precision accuracy. The Hispano-Suiza HS 115-2 is a multi-fuel, liquid-cooled, supercharged V8 engine, which produces 190kW (250hp) at 3,200rpm. It was replaced in 1985 with the Baudouin 6F11 SRX supercharged diesel engine. A pre-selector gearbox with four forward and four reverse gear ratios is used by the AMX-10 RC vehicles. A torque converter is installed in the gearbox, and the clutch is electro-magnetically driven. Fitted with 16 smoke grenade dischargers, the crew can pack 4,000 7.62mm rounds, and 38 main gun rounds into the vehicle. The 105mm gun can fire four types of ammunition, including armour piercing and illumination.

Like the majority of Coalition forces, French commanders ordered extra armour to be fitted to the AMX-10RC for operations in the Gulf War of 1991. Upgrades to the vehicles included a new battlefield management system, called Finders C2R. A further enhancement improved traction on uneven ground and a central tyre inflation mechanism allowed the driver to set pressure in respect of driving conditions.

The AMX-10 RC can perform reconnaissance in a radioactive environment and is fitted with a nuclear, biological, chemical protection system. More than 240 were in use by the French Army in 2021.

AMX-10 RC Armoured Fighting Vehicle Specification	
Model	AMX-10C 30B Armoured Reconnaissance | Fire Support Vehicle
Manufacturer	Nexter Systems
Country	France
Year	1981–to present
Engine	Hispano-Suiza multi-fuel
Fuel	Multi-fuel
Protection	Frontal armour resistant against 23mm API from 300m
Top Speed	35mph (56km/h)
Range	500 miles (804km)
Crew Capacity	Crew of four
Length	30ft
Width	9ft
Height	8ft
Armament	105mm F2 BK MECA L/47
Weight	16 tonnes
Service Branch	French Army

Developed by Nexter Systems, this vehicle type entered service in 1981 and many describe the platform as a 'tank destroyer on wheels'. The AMX-10 RC is typically utilised for fire support in operations where the vehicle supports troops on the ground with sustained fire or engages deliberate targets, as well as mounting reconnaissance missions. (French Armed Forces)

Panhard ERC 90

The ERC 90 is a six-wheeled armoured reconnaissance vehicle equipped with a 90mm gun. A total of 13 vehicles were deployed on the French mission in the Gulf War. The vehicles were tasked to operate ahead of the armoured force collating intelligence and mounting surveillance of Iraq positions. On 24 February 1991, as the ground phase began, reconnaissance units of the 6th French Light Armoured Division advanced into Iraq. The initial objective for the French was an airfield 90 miles inside Iraq at As-Salman.

Right: The ERC 90 is a six-wheeled armoured reconnaissance vehicle equipped with a 90mm gun. A total of 13 vehicles were deployed on the French mission in the Gulf War. (French Armed Forces)

Below: The F4 90mm could fire a round called the Armour Piercing Fin Stabilised Discarding Sabot at a much higher velocity than the Lynx's F1 90mm. GIAT and Panhard claimed it could penetrate heavy armour at 2,000 metres. (French Armed Forces)

Above: On 24 February 1991, as the ground phase began, reconnaissance units of the 6th French Light Armoured Division advanced into Iraq. The initial objective for the French was an airfield 90 miles inside Iraq at As-Salman. (French Armed Forces)

Left: The ERC 90 was used extensively in the Gulf War in support of the infantry. The vehicle could perform reconnaissance in a radioactive environment and was fitted with an NBC protection system. (French Armed Forces)

The French were reinforced by the 325th Airborne Infantry Regiment from the US 82nd Airborne Division, and they quickly crossed the border unopposed and advanced north. By the end of the first day, the French force had secured its objectives and continued the attack north, securing the highways from Baghdad to southern Iraq. The ERC-90 Sagaie was developed for the French Army by Panhard General Defence, while the ERC-90 Lynx was aimed at the export market. Shortly after the ERC 90 F1 Lynx had been built for export, Panhard recognised the need for a cost-effective light armoured vehicle that could defeat a more modern main battle tank (such as the Russian T-72). The ERC-90 Lynx, the export model,

After the conflict, the ERC 90 took part in a number of regional parades across France to mark their service in the Gulf. The ERC 90 force was tasked to operate ahead of the armoured force collating intelligence and mounting surveillance of Iraqi positions. On 24 February 1991, as the ground phase began, reconnaissance units of the 6th French Light Armoured Division advanced into Iraq. (French Armed Forces)

could only fire medium-velocity High Explosive Anti-Tank (HEAT), which lacked the penetration to defeat more modern tanks. Panhard designed a turret that mounted the long barrel F4 90mm smoothbore cannon developed by GIAT, and designated the vehicle the ERC 90 F4 Sagaie. The F4 90mm could fire a round called the APFSDS rounds at a much higher velocity than the Lynx's F1 90mm. GIAT and Panhard claimed it could penetrate heavy armour at 2,000 metres. For a while, GIAT engineers could not find a suitable muzzle brake for the Sagaie, which would not interfere with the firing of APFSDS rounds. They opted to use a muzzle brake design from the older AMX-13 tank.

Panhard ERC Armoured Fighting Vehicle Specification	
Model	Panhard ERC | Armoured Reconnaissance and fire support
Manufacturer	Panhard
Country	France
Year	1980–to present
Engine	Peugeot – V6 Petrol engine 155hp at 5,250rpm
Fuel	Petrol
Protection	14.5mm AP all-around with add-on armour
Top Speed	56mph (90km/h)
Range	450 miles (724km)
Crew Capacity	Crew of three
Length	25ft
Width	8ft
Armament	90mm CN90 cannon
Weight	8.3 tonnes
Service Branch	French Army

VAB – Vehicle de l'Avant Blindé

The French armoured personnel carrier, more commonly known as the VAB, was the primary troop-carrying vehicle deployed to the Gulf War by French forces. The VAB, produced by Renault Trucks, is used by almost every regiment across the Army and the French Foreign Legion. A total of 214 were sent to the Middle East on Operation *Daguet* and used to ferry infantry to their objectives. The VAB is a late Cold War-era armoured personnel carrier built and designed in France. The VAB is a wheeled vehicle with steel monocoque hull – the chassis is integrated with the body. It is produced in a 4x4 and 6x6 configuration, with the 4x4 version being faster on road, cheaper and lighter. The 6x6 version has better off-road performance and can be fitted with heavier weapon systems.

The driver and vehicle commander are seated at the front. The engine is located in the middle and the troop compartment with its large doors and roof hatches is at the rear. The baseline infantry section vehicles are fitted with a small, manually-operated open roof turret with a 12.7mm M2HB heavy machine gun. Other variants are fitted with a 7.5mm AAT-52 or 7.62mm AAT-NF1 machine gun in a small one-man turret. Anti-tank sections could also mount their MILAN or Eryx anti-tank missiles at the rear roof hatches. Various other weapon systems can be fitted, such as 20mm autocannon, HOT anti-tank missiles and mortars. The armour on the VAB is limited in order to retain speed, mobility and amphibious capability. The steel armour is rated against small arms fire and shell splinters. Its tyres are a run-flat design to ensure it can drive out of difficult situations.

An armoured double-door at the rear allows access to the passenger compartment. Two inward-facing, foldable benches provide seating for ten soldiers, five on each side. The crew enters the front compartment through two lateral hatches, the driver on the left and gunner on the right. Additional hatches in the roof give access to armaments and provide emergency exits. The front windows are bulletproof and heated. All windows can be further protected by armoured panels, which can be shut entirely or left as a small observation slit. The engine is located behind the driver, while the right side of the vehicle is kept free, providing a passageway between the crew and passenger compartments. The

Above left: The French armoured personnel carrier, the Vehicle de l'Avant Blindé, more commonly known as the VAB, was the primary troop-carrying vehicle deployed to the Gulf War. It could carry ten fully equipped soldiers and its high ground clearance ensured the good off-road performance that was needed in the desert. (DPL)

Above right: The driver of a VAB stands by his vehicle. His seat is situated at the front of the VAB along with that of the commander. The engine is located in the middle and the large troop compartment with its large doors and roof hatches is at the rear. Rations and water were carried on top of the vehicle. (DPL)

Above left: More than 25 variants of the VAB were produced, which included a command centre, maintenance and recovery, mortar crew with towed weapon trailer, an ambulance fitted with five stretchers, as well as electronic warfare and artillery observation platform. (French Armed Forces)

Above right: The VAB Mephisto (also called VAB HOT) was an anti-tank vehicle with the Euromissile Mephisto system fitted to its roof. It had four ready-to-fire HOT anti-tank missiles and another eight in reserve. (DPL)

upgrade of the VAB with Mexas composite armour aimed at increasing protection against light infantry weapons to protection against heavy machine guns, typically 7.62mm and 12.7mm ammunition. The increased weight of armour, by about two tonnes, cancels the vehicle's amphibious capability. The angular shape of the hull, the relatively light weight and the armour upgrade gave the VAB an improved resistance against mines. When exposed to an explosion from below, the VAB is lifted in the air, allowing the force of the blast to disperse away from the vehicle.

VAB (Véhicule de l'Avant Blindé) Specification	
Model	VAB | Armoured Personnel Carrier | variants
Manufacturer	Renault Trucks Defence
Country	France
Year	1979–to present (upgraded)
Engine	Renault MIDS 062045 235 kW (320hp)
Fuel	Petrol
Protection	Cage, ballistic blanket. Steel armour providing protection against 7.62mm bullets, artillery shell splinters and anti-personnel mines
Top Speed	68mph (109 km/h)
Range	750 miles (1,207km)
Crew Capacity	Two, plus ten passengers
Length	20ft
Width	8ft
Height	7ft
Armament	One AA52 7.62mm machine gun or one 12.7mm heavy machine gun
Weight	14 tonnes
Service Branch	French Army

Chapter 4
Iraq

In 1990, Iraq fielded the world's fifth largest army with 5,500 tanks and more than 10,000 armoured vehicles – although the majority of Baghdad's force was outdated and in need of urgent maintenance. The invasion of Kuwait resulted in an estimated 3,400 Iraqi tanks being destroyed by US and UK tanks. While some of Baghdad's elite tanks' forces fought hard in muzzle-to-muzzle fighting in the Battle for Norfolk – it quickly became apparent that despite the recent war with Iran, which had ended in 1988, the majority of Saddam's tanks crews were not well trained in manoeuvre warfare. Their lack of tactical prowess on the battlefield was evident in the fact that Iraqi commanders ordered some tanks' units into static positions, where they simply acted as tracked artillery. In addition, while on paper Iraq's armour appeared to be a significant strategic threat to the Coalition, Saddam's forces had so many different types of vehicles that spares were in short supply even before the war started. In addition, Iraqi regiments lacked logistics and engineering support, which left vehicles broken down and fuel and ammunition were in short supply on the battlefield.

Tanks

T-72 Main Battle Tank

In the 1991 Gulf War, Iraq's powerful T-72 tank force was a significant concern to Coalition commanders. Saddam's armoured divisions had fought an eight-year war against Iran, and intelligence reports indicated the Republican Guard was well drilled in 'manoeuvre warfare' – a tactic of outflanking an enemy – which Baghdad's forces had used to inflict heavy losses on the Iranians. Among the Iraqi arsenal was a small number of 'home-produced' T-72M1s – a variant built by Iraq and dubbed the 'Lions of Babylon' by the media. However, it turned out that these lions and indeed most of Iraq's main battle tanks had no teeth, at least when pitted against American M1A1 Abrams, the British Challenger, the French AMX-30 and even the older US M-60A3s. During the 1991 conflict, many T-72 crews failed to use their manoeuvrability and instead dug their tanks into fixed defensive positions in the desert making them easy targets for Coalition tanks, which moved across the desert at speed to flank the Iraqi force.

Among Baghdad's arsenal was a small number of T-72M1s – a variant built by Iraq and dubbed the 'Lions of Babylon' by the media. (US Army)

Above: Iraqi defence ministers had visited Russia and purchased the powerful T-72 tank force prior to the invasion of Iraq. Saddam's armoured divisions had fought an eight-year war against Iran and intelligence reports indicated that the Republican Guard was well drilled in 'manoeuvre warfare', which it had used to inflict heavy losses on the Iranians. (DPL)

Right: A destroyed Iraqi T-72 main battle tank. Many of Saddam's elite armoured unit tanks were destroyed by advancing Coalition armoured units. The T-72s had dug into the desert in a defensive line, which made them easy targets for advancing tanks. (US DoD)

There is no question that in 1990, when Saddam's forces invaded Kuwait, the Iraqi Army was well resourced and capable. But while Baghdad could field numerous variants of main battle tanks, armoured personnel carriers and reconnaissance vehicles, there appeared to be little inter-operability between vehicle types such as engines and weapons systems. This made repair and re-supply a challenge with so many different spares needed to support the force. At the start of the conflict, in 1991, the Iraqi Army was able to field five different main battle tanks and more than 15 armoured vehicles, compared to two tanks among US forces and one among British and French, plus a couple of armoured vehicle variants. Unlike Western forces, which invested in one or two vehicle variants, Iraq fielded French, Soviet, Brazilian, Chinese and Yugoslavian armoured vehicles, which offered very little commonality. This put strain on the Army's service support ability to repair and maintain vehicles and may well have been Baghdad's Achilles' heel, forcing many tanks to sit in the sands due to maintenance issues.

The Soviet-designed T-72 main battle tank, served as the backbone of the Iraqi armoured forces during the Iran conflict and the following 1990–91 Gulf War. Developed in the 1960s, the T-72 was known for its battlefield capability, its powerful 125mm smoothbore gun and composite armour.

Iraq acquired a substantial number of T-72 tanks from the Soviet Union in the 1970s and 1980s. Compared to main battle tanks used in the West, the T-72 has a much smaller profile and is lighter at 41 tonnes. It is highly manoeuvrable and could traverse rivers using an installed snorkel allowing the entire tank to submerge. For such evolutions, each member of the crew is equipped with a basic chest-pack rebreather in case of emergency. But if the tank flooded it must have been a terrifying situation. The T-72's engine compartment can flood from pressure loss and if the engine stops underwater, it must be started again in six seconds. The limited space made escape challenging and 'submerge' training exercises were not popular. The tank was also nuclear, biological, and chemical capable – providing a clean air environment for the crew in time of attack.

To reduce penetrating radiation from neutron bomb explosions, boron compound synthetic cloth is used to line the inside of the hull and turret. An air-filter system provides clean air to the crew and a small amount of overpressure keeps contaminants from entering through joints and bearings. The main gun's autoloader facilitates more effective forced smoke removal than conventional manually loaded tank guns, so that, in theory, NBC isolation in the fighting compartment can be maintained forever. Like other Soviet-era tanks, the T-72's design sacrifices interior space to achieve a very thin profile, even going so far as to swap out the fourth crew member for a motorised loader.

The crew height of the T-72 is limited by the low height of the tank; the Soviet Army set a maximum height limit of 5ft 4in for crew members. Even by the restricted standards of battle tanks, the original T-72 design has incredibly small periscope viewports, and when the hatch is closed, the driver's field of vision is very limited. Rather than the more user-friendly steering wheel or steering yoke found in many contemporary Western tanks, the steering system is a dual-tiller arrangement.

The 1973-built turret of the first T-72 is constructed entirely of traditional cast high hardness steel (HHS) armour. Every upgrade to the tank saw improvements to the T-72's armour protection. The front plate measures 3.1in, and the maximum thickness is estimated to be 11in. Because of their failure to mount effective armoured warfare in the 1991 Gulf War, some tanks were primarily used in an armoured self-propelled artillery role. Where T-72s did engage they fought well, but according to Coalition commanders, the Iraqi T-72's performance was poor.

In one example, a US Army M1 Abrams main battle tank, firing a 120mm depleted uranium (DU) APFSDS round destroyed a T-72 tank at a range of more than 2,000 metres, while Iraq's APFSDS 125mm round had an effective range of just 1,800 metres. On 27 February 1991, M60A1s from 1st Marine Division, codenamed 'Task Force Ripper', led the drive to Kuwait International Airport. About 100 Iraqi tanks and armoured personnel carriers, including T-72 tanks, were destroyed by the USMC's M60A1 tanks. At the end of the war, it was estimated that more than 150 Iraqi T-72s were lost. T-72s did account for at least two M2 Bradley kills – both on 26 February 1991 – and left several damaged. Overall, the T-72 offered little challenge to Abrams and Challenger tanks.

The blackened hulks of T-72s hit by Coalition air power and armour as they sat waiting in the desert. Their lack of manoeuvrability baffled Western commanders, who later discovered the tanks had little fuel and were in urgent need of a serious maintenance. (US DoD)

T-72 – Main Battle Tank (numerous variants) Specification	
Model	T-72 Main Battle Tank
Manufacturer	Soviet Union (Russia) Kartsev-Venediktov and Lion of Babylon project
Country	Iraq
Year	1989–90
Engine	V-12 diesel 780hp
Fuel	Diesel
Protection	Steel and composite armour with ERA
Top Speed	40mph (64km/h)
Range	290 miles (466km), extends to 430 miles with external fuel drums (692km)
Crew Capacity	Crew of three
Length	31ft
Width	12ft
Height	7ft
Armament	125mm 2A46M/2A46M-5 smoothbore gun, support from 12.7mm heavy machine gun
Weight	41 tonnes
Service Branch	Iraqi Army

The T-72 was known for its battlefield capability, its powerful 125mm smoothbore gun and composite armour. Iraq had acquired a substantial number of T-72 tanks from the Soviet Union in the 1970s and 1980s, but the Iraqis failed to use the tanks to advantage and many were destroyed. (US DoD)

In 1991, the T-72 was seen as a significant threat to the Coalition. Compared to main battle tanks used in the West, the T-72 has a much smaller profile, was lighter at 41 tonnes and much more manoeuvrable. The Iraqi Army did not take advantage of these benefits. (US DoD)

T-62 Main Battle Tank

Iraq's armoured brigades operated the T-62s in large numbers, but the tank lacked high-powered optics, thermal sights and basic computer technology compared to its adversaries in 1991. The Iraqi's 3rd Armoured Division alone lost 110 of its T-62 tank force. The T-62 medium tank, known under the Soviet identification of Object 166, officially entered service in the Soviet Army in August 1961. The tank was designed and built at Factory No. 183 in Nizhniy Tagil, known as Uralvagonzavod. The vehicle was developed as a direct response to the then new American M60 tank, which had been dispatched to the 3rd Armoured Division to serve with the US Army in Europe in December 1960.

The design of the T-62 was an amalgamation of several existing concepts that had previously remained at the experimental stage, but nevertheless were already well established before the M60 was known in the USSR. In addition to the research work that had been accumulated since the start of a new Soviet medium-tank programme in 1953, several more years were spent shaping the T-62 into its final design. Many components, from communications to lighting were adopted as standard from previous tanks.

The crew of a T-62 was equipped with the same controls and observation devices as those used in the T-55 counterparts. The driver was provided with two periscopes, laid out to ensure that he could see both front corners of the hull. He could swap out one periscope for a night-vision periscope, which could also be mounted externally when driving from an open hatch. The loader had a single rotating periscope for a relatively restricted view to the left side of the turret. The gunner was provided with a single forward-facing periscope for general observation and to alleviate sickness, which could be a problem when the tank was locked down and the gunner had no vision. His main observation device was a telescopic sight, known as the TSh2B-41.

The on-board fuel carried in a T-62 was divided between four internal Bakelite-coated steel tanks, holding a total of 148 gallons, and three external tanks on the fenders with a capacity of 60 gallons. Additionally, a pair of external fuel drums could be mounted on to the rear of the hull for extended range – a tactic used on many Soviet tanks.

The T-62 was the first production tank equipped with a smoothbore tank gun that could fire armour-piercing stabilised rounds at a greater velocity than earlier tanks, which has used rifled tank guns. Due to its greater manufacturing costs and maintenance requirements than its predecessor, the T-62 did not completely replace the T-55 in export markets, even though it became the standard tank in the Soviet arsenal.

Above left: **The T-62 was a Soviet main battle tank, first introduced in 1961. The tank was an upgrade of the T-55 and retained many similar design elements of its predecessor including low profile and thick turret armour. In this image, the driver's and commander's hatches can clearly be seen. (US Army)**

Above right: **A T-62 abandoned on the main road linking Kuwait to the Iraq border. In contrast with previous tanks, which were armed with rifled guns, the T-62 was the first production tank armed with a smoothbore gun that could fire armour-piercing rounds. (US Army).**

Inside the T-62, space was at a premium. The driver's compartment was in the lower front, the fighting compartment in the middle, and the engine compartment at the back. The loader, gunner, driver and commander made up the crew of four. The tank had capacity to carry 40 'immediate use' rounds with additional rounds kept in storage in the front of the hull, to the right of the driver, and in the rear of the fighting compartment. On operations, four rounds were kept in the turret. The coaxial machine gun's 2,500 rounds were also stored inside.

The T-62 was less manoeuvrable than the T-55 because of its increased weight. After war with Iran, Saddam boosted his armoured capability importing nearly 3,000 Chinese tanks. By the start of the Gulf War, the T-62 had lost much of its prominence in the Iraqi Army, making up less than one-sixth of its tank fleet, but nevertheless, it took part in the fight against Coalition forces in 1991. Its performance was poor, like the T-72, it appeared to have lacked maintenance while its crews lacked motivation and many quickly surrendered.

T-62 – Main Battle Tank (numerous variants) Specification	
Model	T-62 | Main Battle Tank | variants
Manufacturer	Soviet Union (Russia) Uralvagonzavod
Country	Iraq
Year	1961–present
Engine	V-12 diesel 780hp (582kw)
Fuel	Diesel
Protection	Heavy protected turret and upper side with 153mm steel
Top Speed	31mph (50km/h)
Range	280 miles (450km)
Crew Capacity	Four
Length	30ft
Width	11ft
Height	8ft
Armament	Main gun 115mm smoothbore U-5TS (2A20) barrel, support from 12.7mm heavy machine gun and 7.62 PKT coaxial machine gun
Weight	37 tonnes
Service Branch	Iraqi Army

A burnt-out Iraqi T-62 north of Kuwait City. Then commander's and gunner's cupolas have been left open and damage to the rear of the tank suggests it was attacked from behind, possibly by an artillery round. Ancillary boxes for crew equipment can be seen on the left-hand side of the T-62.

T-55

Iraq fielded hundreds of T-55 tanks, which were assigned to the 10th and 12th Armoured Divisions. The tanks had spearheaded the invasion of Kuwait and in January and February of 1991, Iraqi T-55s were deployed in the desert to counter any coalition breakout. They lacked heavy armour, which left the crews vulnerable and when the T-55s were in action against the more advanced coalition tanks, they faced formidable challenges. The coalition was able to effectively engage and destroy Iraqi T-55 tanks because they possessed sophisticated armament, including thermal-imaging systems, precision-guided munitions, and better reconnaissance capabilities.

One of the most extensively manufactured tanks of the Cold War era was the T-55. It had been constructed by the Soviet Union and went into service in the late 1940s and deployed in the post-war years. Its primary weapon was a 100mm gun, listed as the D-10T-TS2. It is capable of firing high-explosive, armour-piercing, and shaped-charge ammunition, with a maximum indirect fire mission range of 1.46km.

The right side of the main gun is a 7.62mm SGMT coaxial machine gun, while the driver can fire a remote-controlled weapon positioned in the middle of the glacis plate by pressing a button on the right steering lever. The driver sits in the front, the combat compartment is in the middle, and the engine and gearbox are located in the back of the T-55's all-welded steel hull. A single piece hatch that swings to the left is provided for the driver, at the front of the tank. In front of this hatch are two day periscopes, one of which may be switched out for an infrared periscope, which is utilised in tandem with the infrared light that is fixed on the right side of the glacial plate. There is a turntable in the combat compartment to assist the lack of space.

The Iraqi T-55s lacked engine upgrades that effectively reduced its capability. The tank can wade through water to a maximum depth of 4ft and carries the relevant equipment to cross a much deeper river or stream with the maximum depth – using a snorkel – being 16ft. The snorkel is fitted over the loader's hatch cover and when not in use, the snorkel is disassembled and placed behind the hull or turret in specific storage rack. The T-55 carried smoke-generating machinery to create a screen or shield to

Above left: Iraq fielded hundreds of T-55 tanks, which were assigned to the 10th and 12th Armoured Divisions. The tanks had spearheaded the invasion of Kuwait and in January and February of 1991, Iraqi T-55s were deployed in the desert to counter any Coalition break-out. (US DoD)

Above right: An Iraqi T-55 abandoned by its crew on a highway between Basra and Kuwait City in 1991. The T-55 was one of the most extensively manufactured tanks of the Cold War era; it had been constructed by the Soviet Union and went into service in the late 1940s. Its primary weapon was a 100mm gun, listed as the D-10T-TS2. (US DoD)

hide from an adversary. It functions by injecting fuel into the exhaust manifolds causing it to combine with exhaust gases and generate smoke. Despite the potent main armament, the T-55 delivered a poor performance in the 1991 Gulf conflict. Many commanders failed to manoeuvre their force across the desert and instead fixed themselves in defensive positions.

T-55 – Main Battle Tank (Numerous Variants) Specification	
Model	T-55 | Main Battle Tank | variants
Manufacturer	Soviet Union (Russia) KhPZ, UVZ
Country	Iraq
Year	1948–present
Engine	Model V-55 V12 water cooled 38.88 litre diesel 500hp
Fuel	Diesel
Protection	Heavy-protected turret (205mm) and upper side (79mm)
Top Speed	32mph (51km/h)
Range	202 miles (325km)
Crew Capacity	Four
Length	29ft
Width	11ft
Height	8ft
Armament	Main gun 115mm smoothbore U-5TS (2A20) barrel, support from 12.7mm heavy machine gun and 7.62 PKT coaxial machine gun
Weight	37 tonnes
Service Branch	Iraqi Army

Above left: Like most MBTs, T-55s could have external fuel tanks attached to extend their fuel range from 200 to 380 miles. Most carried two drums at the rear – this tank appears to have lost one, a second can be seen at the rear of the tank. (DPL)

Above right: A burnt out T-55s in the desert during the 1991 war. Hundreds of T-55 were destroyed in the conflict. These tanks were some of the oldest MBTs in Iraq's inventory. They lacked heavy armour, which left crews vulnerable and when the T-55s were in action against the more advanced Coalition tanks, they faced formidable challenges. (DPL)

Type 59

China sold hundreds of the Type 59 main battle tanks to Iraq in the late 1980s after Baghdad's war with Iran. It saw service during the Gulf War in 1990–91. The Type 59 was a Chinese-manufactured variant of the Soviet T-54A tank, which was an early model of the widely used T-54/55 series – many of which look very similar. With a cast dome-shaped gun turret in the centre of the hull and an engine compartment at the back, the Type 59 features a typical post-war configuration. The hull is made of welded steel, with thicknesses ranging from paper thin on the hull floor to more than 4in thick on the front lower glacis.

Like most Soviet tanks, the Chinese copies positioned the driver's seat on the front left side of the hull, and a hatch just above it that opens to the left. When buttoned up, the driver's two pop-up vision blocks provide coverage ahead and to the right. Together with the loader and gunner, the commander occupied the turret. The gunner sits in front of and below the commander's feet, and the loader is positioned to the right of the turret in a restricted space. The non-rotating floor of the turret makes it difficult for the crew to operate in the confined area.

A rifled 100mm Type 59 gun was fitted to the Type 59 and most crews carried 34 rounds. A secondary close-quarter weapon, a 7.62mm machine gun positioned to the right of the main armament and above the gunner's hatch is a Type 54 12.7mm anti-aircraft machine gun, which holds 200 rounds. It is the Chinese version of the Russian 12.7mm DShKM heavy machine gun.

The Type 59 was powered by V-12 liquid-cooled diesel engine supported by a manual gearbox with five forward and one reverse gear. An internal fuel tank holds up to 200 gallons of diesel, while an external fuel tank can hold another 60 gallons.

Because ammunition is kept inside the turret, it has very little resilience to enemy firepower should it penetrate the hull, which risks a secondary explosion of stored ammunition. During Operation *Desert Storm*, a number of Iraqi Type 59s that were engaged by Western armour erupted with a second explosion due to the ammunition detonating.

Above left: **China sold hundreds of Types 59 main battle tanks to Iraq in the late 1980s after Baghdad's war with Iran. The type saw service during the Gulf War in 1990–91. (French Armed Forces)**

Above right: **The Type 59 was powered by a V-12 liquid-cooled diesel engine and was supported by a manual gearbox with five forward and one reverse gears. An internal fuel tank could hold up to 200 gallons of diesel, while an external fuel tank could hold an additional 60 gallons. (French Armed Forces)**

T-59 – Main Battle Tank (Chinese Version of the Soviet T-54) Specification	
Model	T-59 | Main Battle Tank | variants
Manufacturer	China – First Inner Mongolia Machinery Factory, Norinco
Country	Iraq
Year	1959–present
Engine	Model 12150L V-12 liquid-cooled diesel 520hp (390kW)
Fuel	Diesel
Protection	20–203mm steel armour
Top Speed	32mph (51km/h)
Range	280 miles (450km)
Crew Capacity	Four
Length	20ft
Width	11ft
Height	9ft
Armament	Main gun 100mm rifled gun. Supported by two Type 59T 7.62mm coaxial machine guns, Type 54 12.7mm air-defence machine guns
Weight	36 tonnes
Service Branch	Iraqi Army

Type 69

A first-generation Chinese main battle tank, the Type 69 was an improvement on the Type 59. The People's Republic of China supplied Iraq with more than 1,500 Type 69 MBTs in the 1980s and the Iraqi Army designated them as Type 69-QM. The Iraqi Type 69-QM was fitted with a 100mm rifled gun as standard and a secondary coaxial machine gun, along with a 12.7mm anti-aircraft machine gun. According to Western observers, Iraq modified some Type 69s with a 105mm cannon, a 60mm mortar, and a 125mm gun with an autoloader prior to the Persian Gulf War in 1990–91. During the Gulf War in 1991, Iraqi Type 69 units were said to have performed well and appeared to have been maintained.

There was little visual difference between the Type 59 and Type 69. The gun's fume extractor was repositioned a little, and the turret was fitted with a sizable infrared light. It was the first Chinese tank that could fight at night using a tiny infrared light on the commander's hatch and a laser rangefinder on the gun mantlet – the armoured plate to the side of the gun.

USMC personnel inspect an abandoned Iraqi Type 69-QM, Main Battle Tank. This was a first-generation Chinese main battle tank; the Type 69 was an improvement on the Type 59. The People's Republic of China (PLA) supplied Iraq with more than 1,500 Type 69 MBTs in the 1980s which the Iraqi Army designated as Type 69-QM. (US Army)

It was the first tank in China to be equipped with a 100mm smoothbore gun – allowing it to fire armour-piercing fin stabilised rounds and it had a limited gun stabilisation system. Interestingly, while Coalition forces feared a chemical warfare attack from the Iraqi force, the Type 59 lacked any NBC protection.

Type 69 – Main Battle Tank (Specification)	
Model	Type-69 | Main Battle Tank
Manufacturer	China – First Inner Mongolia Machinery Factory, Norinco
Country	Iraq
Year	1959–present
Engine	12150L-7 V-12 diesel engine 580hp (430kW)
Fuel	Diesel
Protection	203mm
Top Speed	30mph (48km/h)
Range	270 miles (434km)
Crew Capacity	Four
Length	20ft
Width	10ft
Height	9ft
Armament	Main gun 100mm smoothbore/105mm rifled
Weight	36 tonnes
Service Branch	Iraqi Army

Above left: An abandoned Iraqi Type 69 on fire and pictured abandoned on a highway outside Kuwait City The Type 69-QM was the first tank in China to be equipped with a 100mm smoothbore gun – allowing it to fire armour-piercing fin stablised rounds. It also had a limited gun stabilisation system. (DPL)

Above right: British troops inspect the remains of what appears to be a destroyed Iraqi Type 69 on the edge of oil fields, which Saddam forces set ablaze. The tank pictured is badly damaged. There was little visual difference between the Type 59 and Type 69. The gun's fume extractor was repositioned a little, and the turret was fitted with a sizable infrared light. (DPL)

Armoured Vehicles

BMP-1

Iraq adopted the Soviet Union's BMP-1 amphibious tracked infantry personnel carrier for its forces. It was widely deployed by Saddam's forces in Kuwait and across the desert – its low profile was a considerable advantage, but it lacked heavy firepower and its limited armour left the vehicle vulnerable. When the BMP was originally designed in the late 1950s, it was required to be fast, have a powerful weapon, and allow every squad member to shoot from inside the vehicle – using portholes that allowed soldiers to fire from the confines of a protected vehicle. The armament needed to be able to defeat similar small armoured vehicles as well as directly help infantry that was dismounted in both the attack and defence. The vehicle was required to protect the crew from light shell fragments at 500–800 metres away, as well as heavy machine-gun fire. As Western weapon technology improved, the BMP became exposed.

Iraq purchased more than 800 BMP-2s and about 1,000 BMP-1s in the late 1970s from Moscow. In a move to improve the armour, Iraqi commanders upgraded the BMP, which was known as the Saddam 1. Engineers added appliqué armour to the sides of the hull to improve protection, but the additional armour was too heavy for the chassis, the engine and the gearbox. The Saddam 1 was never put into production.

The second improvement, called the Saddam II, included more armour on the top hull sides, and a rubber side skirt. In contrast to the previous modification, it was put into production and was primarily utilised by the Republican Guard. Firepower was provided by an anti-tank wire-guided missile (ATGM) launcher and a 73mm 2A28 Grom cannon, which had been used on multiple Soviet vehicles. The gun's planned range was listed at 1,100 yards, which was deemed sufficient to engage enemy armoured vehicles and ground forces. The missile launcher was designed to be employed against close range targets as the

Above left: Iraq purchased more than 800 BMP-2s and about 1,000 BMP-1s in the late 1970s from Moscow. In a move to improve the armour, Iraqi commanders upgraded the BMP, which was known as the Saddam 1. Engineers added appliqué armour to the sides of the hull to improve protection, but it was too heavy for the chassis, the engine and the gearbox. (US Army)

Above right: The driver is seated in the front with an ammunition stowage behind his seat. When this hatch is closed, he has three periscope vision-blocks to help him see. The BMP was the first armoured vehicle from the Soviet Union to employ a basic yoke steering system. (US Army)

vehicle advanced towards the frontline. The BMP-1 featured an electric traverse drive with a manual back-up mechanism and a fume-extractor system installed in its conical turret. There is a dead-zone over the commander's hatch where the main cannon must be raised over the infrared searchlight to prevent crushing it. Hatches above the troop compartment cannot open while the gun is aimed backwards.

On the left side of the hull, the driver is seated in the front. When his hatch is closed, he has three periscope vision-blocks to help him see. The BMP was the first armoured vehicle from the Soviet Union to employ a basic yoke steering system. The BMP-1's sharply sloping frontal armour was able to withstand small arms fire, but not heavier anti-tank and artillery rounds. Many Iraqi crews lacked training and understanding of the BMP's capability.

BMP-2

The BMP-2M was an improved version of the BMP-2 and provided increased mobility and firepower. It was popular with Iraqi troops particularly as the crew benefited from an air conditioning system – when it worked. The vehicle carried three crew members, including a driver, gunner, and commander as well as seven soldiers in the troop compartment. A 30mm automatic grenade launcher (AGL), a 7.62mm PKT coaxial machine gun, and a 30mm automatic gun were mounted on the turret. The 7.62mm gun could fire 2,000 rounds per minute. This equated to 500 7.62mm bullets leaving the gun every 15 seconds – after 10,000 rounds the gunner often had to change the barrel as it got too hot. The heavier 30mm cannon could fire at rate of 500 rounds per minute. The AGL has a maximum range of 2,500 yards and was able to launch 250 grenades per minute. According to the designers of the BMP, the KBP Instrument Design Bureau, the vehicle was able to withstand high-explosive anti-tank (HEAT) missiles and 12.7mm B-3232 rounds thanks to its appliqué armour protecting its hull. A multi-channel optical system was fitted to the BMP-2 to stabilise the field of view during operations. To increase target identification accuracy and mission efficiency, the vehicle carried a thermal-imaging system, a laser rangefinder, and an advanced target-detection system. Powered by a six-cylinder, four-stroke, supercharged, direct-injection diesel engine, the BMP-2M was a much-improved version of the BMP1. It had a reputation of being

Above left: Iraqi BMP-2 on the move outside of Kuwait. Iraqi forces swept through Kuwait on their initial invasion due to a lack of preparedness and firepower from Kuwaiti forces. (US DoD)

Above right: BMP-2 were used in Iraq by Iraqi forces. Here Georgian Defence Force soldiers prepare to move a BMP-2 Infantry Fighting Vehicle during the *Agile Spirit 19* closing ceremony live-fire exercise on 9 August 2019, in Georgia. (US DoD)

The Soviet BMP-2 improved numerous features including a new main gun. (US DoD)

A captured Iraqi BMP-2 sits at the United States Army Ordnance Museum. (US DoD)

BMP-2M undergoing engine maintenance as part of the Western Military District. (US DoD)

indestructible and in the Persian Gulf Iraqi-commanders were convinced the vehicle would outperform Western forces. They were wrong and today, many rusting hulks of the BMP-2 remain in the desert.

BMP-1 (2) – Armoured Infantry Fighting Vehicle Specification		BMP-2 Specification
Model	BMP-1 infantry fighting vehicle (Soviet Union)	BMP-2 infantry fighting vehicle (Soviet Union)
Manufacturer	Kurganmashzavod (Soviet Union) and ZTS Detva Designed by Pavel Isakov Design Bureau	Kurganmashzavod, Ordnance Factory Medak
Country	Iraq	
Year	1966–present	1979–present
Engine	UTD-20 V6 diesel engine 300hp (224kW) at 2,600rpm	Diesel UTD-20/3 300hp
Fuel	Diesel	Diesel
Protection	Welded rolled steel (33mm)	33mm
Top Speed	40mph (64km/h)	40mph 64km/h)
Range	350 miles (563km)	370 miles (595km)
Crew Capacity	Three, plus eight passengers	Three, plus seven passengers
Length	22ft	22ft
Width	10ft	10ft
Height	7ft	8ft
Armament	One 73mm 2A28 smoothbore gun and or 9MI4 Malyutka ATGM	30mm 2A42 autocannon 9M113 Konkurs ATGM
Weight	13 tonnes	14 tonnes
Service Branch	Iraqi Army	

BMP-2M undergoing routine maintenance in the Western Military District. Maintenance is essential to keeping these machines running in their best condition possible, something Iraq failed to do with most of its equipment. (US DoD)

AMX-10P

The AMX-10P was a French-built amphibious infantry fighting vehicle procured by Iraq in the early 1980s. It had been introduced by Paris to replace the French Army's AMX-VCI and, in contrast to the vehicle it replaced, the AMX-10P was a standalone vehicle that didn't have any shared components. Its aluminium armour plates were soldered together to form the hull. Heavy armour at the front protected against heavy calibre rounds. The turret front had four smoke dischargers for active protection and the vehicle was fitted with a chemical warfare protection system to safeguard the crew. A searchlight, which could be deployed on each side, was also fitted to the turret. The driver sat in the front left and had two viewing periscopes. The infantry, seated on individual bucket seats, had room for heavy back packs. The electric ramp was the main troop exit and, if needed, two roof hatches were available.

The turret housed both the commander and gunner, operating a low-profile 20mm GIAT M693 automatic cannon and a coaxial 7.62mm AA52 machine gun. The vehicle could carry Euromissile MILAN launchers and had variants such as the PAC-90 tank destroyer with a 90mm high-velocity gun.

The AMX-10P was a French-built amphibious infantry fighting vehicle procured by Iraq in the early 1980s. The turret front had four smoke dischargers for active protection and the vehicle was fitted with a chemical warfare protection system to safeguard the crew. (French Armed Forces)

The AMX-10P underwent several upgrades during its lifespan, including a more powerful engine, reinforced gearbox, and modified suspensions for additional armour. The AMX-10P was fully amphibious, with rear water jet propellers and a front trim vane for swimming. (French Armed Forces)

Powered by a Hispano-Suiza HS 115 diesel engine, the AMX-10P had a top speed of 40mph and 8 knots on water. The vehicle underwent several upgrades including a more powerful engine, reinforced gearbox, and modified suspensions for additional armour. The AMX-10P was fully amphibious with rear water jet propellers and a front trim vane for swimming. Iraqi forces used the AMX-10P in a logistic support role, but maintenance was a problem due to sanctions that prevented spares being supplied and a lack of engineering conformity with other armoured vehicles.

AMX-10P – Armoured Infantry Fighting Vehicle (Amphibious Capable) Specification	
Model	AMX-10P
Manufacturer	GIAT Industries France
Country	Built by France, in service with Iraq
Year	1973–94
Engine	Hispano-Suiza | Model 115-2 eight-cylinder liquid-cooled diesel 275hp
Fuel	Diesel
Protection	Welded rolled steel (33mm)
Top Speed	40mph (64km/h)
Range	370 miles (595km)
Crew Capacity	Three, plus eight passengers
Length	19ft
Width	9ft
Height	6ft
Armament	One 20mm F2/M693 auto cannon
Weight	14 tonnes
Service Branch	Iraqi Army

The turret housed both the commander and gunner, operating a low-profile 20mm GIAT M693 automatic cannon and a coaxial 7.62mm AA52 machine gun. The vehicle could carry Euromissile MILAN launchers and had variants such as the PAC-90, and a 90mm high-velocity gun. (French Armed Forces)

Panhard AML

The Panhard AML reconnaissance armoured car was yet another French platform that Iraq had procured long before the invasion of Kuwait. Designed on a 4×4 chassis and weighing approximately 5.5 tonnes, the Panhard was deployed in small numbers with many being held back in Baghdad as part of a reserve force. The Panhard AML had the appearance of the British Army's Ferret Scout car – only much bigger and with a 90mm rifled cannon. The AML was powered by a four-cylinder engine inspired by the Panhard EBR. It was air-cooled and many claimed it was underpowered for its weight. The hull is assembled from 13 welded pieces, featuring a cramped turret basket, which is very restricted due to the presence of the gun breech. The turret has a two-man crew, with the commander on the left and gunner on the right. During the 1991 Gulf War, Iraqi forces equipped with the AML operated in a reconnaissance role. An Iraqi-armoured reconnaissance platoon could consist of up to eight AMLs. At the Battle of Khafaji in 1991, AML-90s engaged USMC and Saudi National Guard units with little effect. The US estimated Iraq operated 300 AMLs in 1990, losing about half during the Gulf War. Despite some remaining in service in 2003, Iraqi AMLs faced challenges due to erratic maintenance and a lack of spare parts. They clashed with American tanks during the invasion of Iraq in 2003 in the vicinity of Nasiriyah.

Panhard AML – Armoured Reconnaissance Vehicle (Amphibious Capable) Specification		
Model	Panhard AML 60	Panhard AML 90
Manufacturer	Panhard – France	
Country	Iraq	
Year	1960–87	1960–85
Engine	Panhard 1.99L Model 4 HD flat 4-cylinder air-cooled petrol	Panhard gasoline, 1.99L Mod.4HD 4-cylinder water-cooled 90hp
Fuel	Petrol	
Protection	Welded rolled steel (33mm)	18mm steel
Top Speed	62mph (99km/h)	65mph (104km/h)
Range	370 miles (595km)	250 miles (402km)
Crew Capacity	Three	Three
Length	17ft	17ft
Width	7ft	6ft
Height	7ft	7ft
Armament	One 90mm D921/GIAT F1 – supported by 7.62mm coaxial machine gun	90mm GIAT F1 (20 rounds) (4in) 7.62mm MAS coaxial 3200 rounds
Weight	5 tonnes	6 tonnes
Service Branch	Iraqi Army	

The Panhard AML reconnaissance armoured car was another French platform that Iraq had procured long before the invasion of Kuwait. Access was via the side door or roof hatches. The vision blocks used by the driver when the hatch is closed can be seen just below the barrel. (French Armed Forces)

Designed on a 4×4 chassis and weighing approximately 5.5 tonnes, the Panhard was deployed in small numbers with many being held back in Baghdad as part of a reserve force. The Panhard AML had the appearance of the British Army's Ferret scout car – only much bigger and with a 90mm rifled cannon. (French Armed Forces)

EE-9 Cascavel

The six-wheeled EE-9 Cascavel armoured reconnaissance vehicle was purchased by Iraq from Brazil in the 1980s. On flat, hard sand, the Cascavel was able to out-manoeuvre Coalition combat vehicles, at least on paper. However, while the wheeled vehicle drove well on hard sand, it struggled in the soft sand of the open desert, which was more suited to tracked vehicles. The Cascavel stood high and was often referred to as Iraq's armoured boat. The vehicle had a steep frontal glacis – the sloped frontmost section of the hull of a tank – designed to counter any small arms fire. The hull sides were almost vertical and vulnerable to missile attack. The EE-9 design also incorporated a low, well-rounded turret on the forward section of the hull with a long, tapered gun barrel and a triple baffle muzzle brake. All Cascavel variants shared a common layout, featuring the driver positioned at the front left, a central turret and the motor and transmission at the rear. The upgraded Cascavel Mk III was armed with an Engesa 90mm gun. Its secondary armament was a coaxial 7.62mm machine gun. Iraq had acquired more than 400 Brazilian-made Cascavel vehicles; they were regarded as easy and cheap to maintain, but by the time the US-led Coalition ejected Saddam's military from Kuwait, Baghdad had still not paid for them.

The Cascavel stood high and was often referred to as Iraqi's armoured boat. The vehicle had a steep frontal glacis – the sloped frontmost section of the hull of a tank – designed to counter any small arms fire. (French Armed Forces)

EE-9 Cascavel – Armoured Reconnaissance Vehicle Specification	
Model	EE-9 Cascavel – Armoured Reconnaissance Vehicle
Manufacturer	Engesa | Brazil
Country	Iraq
Year	1974–93
Engine	Detroit Diesel six-cylinder water-cooled. Automatic transmission
Fuel	Petrol
Protection	Welded rolled steel (33mm)
Top Speed	62mph (99km/h)
Range	470 miles (756km)
Crew Capacity	Crew of three
Length	21ft
Width	9ft
Height	9ft
Armament	90mm Engesa EC-90
Weight	12 tonnes
Service Branch	Iraqi Army

The six-wheeled EE-9 Cascavel armoured reconnaissance vehicle was purchased by Iraq from Brazil in the 1980s. The EE9 Cascavel formed part of the reconnaissance force, but many suffered a direct hit from Coalition forces. The picture shows an EE9 which appears to have been in a static position and fell victim to Coalition firepower. (French Armed Forces)

EE-3 Jararaca

Baghdad's defence procurement relationship with Brazil in the 1980s resulted in the purchase of a second reconnaissance vehicle, the EE-3 Jararaca. It was designed for internal security, liaison, and route reconnaissance. The Jararaca is a 4x4 with hydraulic absorbers and springs combined for independent suspension on each wheel. The vehicle can operate in extreme terrain. The Jararaca's driver sits in the centre at the front and has three periscopes mounted on his roof hatch to cover the vehicle's front arc.

Positioned on the right side behind the driving compartment, the commander's rotatable cupola is equipped with three periscopes for observation. The observer is the third person in the crew. He has a separate access hatch and is seated to the commander's left. The observer also controls the weapon system in certain configurations. A left side entrance and the individual hatches allow the crew to enter the vehicle. Every Jararaca comes with a night-vision device and a radio set. There are automatic fire extinguishers in the engine and fighting compartments. The vehicle is powered by a Mercedes-Benz diesel engine, which supports speeds of up to 45mph.

EE-3 Jararaca – Armoured Scout Car Specification	
Model	EE-3 Jararaca
Manufacturer	Engesa | Brazil
Country	Iraq
Year	1982–90
Engine	Mercedes-Benz OM 314A 4-cylinder, water-cooled diesel 120hp
Fuel	Petrol
Protection	Welded rolled steel (33mm)
Top Speed	62mph (99km/h)
Range	470 miles (756km)
Crew Capacity	Three
Length	14ft
Width	7ft
Height	5ft
Armament	12.7mm M2 Browning machine gun
Weight	6 tonnes
Service Branch	Iraqi Army

Baghdad's growing relationship with Brazil in the 1980s resulted in the procurement of a second reconnaissance vehicle, the EE-3 Jararaca. It was designed for internal security, liaison, and route reconnaissance. The Jararaca is a 4x4 with hydraulic absorbers and springs combined for independent suspension on each wheel. (French Armed Forces)

BRDM-2

The Soviet Union's BRDM-2 was a combat reconnaissance vehicle manned by a crew of four and with a reputation for reliability. The BRDM-2 was equipped with a single-man turret mounted in the centre of the vehicle. The turret weapon was a 14.5mm KPVT heavy machine gun with a coaxial 7.62 PKT machine gun to its right side. A telescopic sight is mounted to the left of the main armament. The day-only sight is provided with a wiper. The turret has a manual traverse and is provided with an adjustable seat for the gunner. The all-welded steel armour hull of the BRDM-2 provides the crew with protection from small arms fire of 7.62mm calibre and shell splinters.

The driver is seated at the front of the hull on the left with the vehicle commander to his right. Both are provided with a bulletproof windscreen to their front, which is covered by an armoured shutter, hinged at the top, when the vehicle is in combat areas. When the shutters are in position, the driver and commander observe the terrain through day periscopes around the front and sides of their positions, mounted level with the roof of the vehicle. The crew mounts and dismounts the vehicle via two hatches over the driver and commander stations.

There is one firing port on each side of the hull and immediately behind it are three day-vision blocks. The engine compartment is at the rear of the hull and there are two air-inlet louvres in the forward part of the engine compartment roof and four more to the rear. The exhaust pipes are on each side of the hull. The

The Soviet Union BRDM-2 was a combat reconnaissance vehicle manned by a crew of four and had a reputation for reliability. The BRDM-2 is equipped with a single-man turret mounted in the centre of the vehicle. The turret is armed with one 14.5mm KPVT heavy machine gun and a coaxial 7.62 PKT machine gun on the right side. (US Army)

The all-welded steel armour hull of the BRDM-2 provides the crew with protection from small arms fire of 7.62mm calibre and shell splinters. The driver is seated at the front of the hull on the left with the vehicle commander to his right. (US Army)

vehicle can accommodate up to five military personnel. The BRDM-2 features an over-pressure collective NBC filtration system, four Infra-Red (IR) driving lights, and an IR spotlight, which is fitted to the right of the commander's hatch. The turret permits an elevation of the armament to more than 30 degrees. There is an air inlet on the hull top on the left side of the turret. Additionally, the ceiling of the engine compartment has four smaller air-inlets to the rear and two larger ones in the forward section. There are strategically located vision blocks on both sides. The welded steel armour of the vehicle is designed to withstand small arms fire and fragments of shells, but it is insufficient to protect against large artillery fragments or .50-calibre machine-gun fire, which can pierce the maximum armour of the BRDM-2.

BRDM 2 – Armoured Reconnaissance Vehicle Specification	
Model	BRDM
Manufacturer	Gorky Automobile Plant (Soviet)
Country	Iraq
Year	1962–89
Engine	Gaz 41 gasoline V8 140hp
Fuel	Petrol
Protection	Welded rolled steel (2–14mm)
Top Speed	62mph (99km/h)
Range	470 miles (756km)
Crew Capacity	Four
Length	18ft
Width	8ft
Height	8ft
Armament	14.5mm KPVT heavy machine gun
Weight	7 tonnes
Service Branch	Iraqi Army

The vehicle can accommodate up to five military personnel. The BRDM-2 features an over pressure collective NBC filtration system, four Infra-Red (IR) driving lights, and an IR spotlight, which is fitted to the right of the commander's hatch. There is one firing port on each side of the hull and immediately behind it are three day-vision blocks. (US Army)

Panhard M3

The Panhard M3 was introduced in 1971 and was another French purchase. This wheeled, armoured vehicle could carry ten soldiers and performed surprisingly well in the desert. The M3's hull was made entirely of welded steel. Like the AML, the hull features a horizontal roofline, and a pointed tapering front. To deflect the blast of a landmine, the bottom of the hull construction is welded to a shallow V-shape. Located right behind the driver is the engine and gearbox. Exhaust pipes run on each side of the roofline, and intakes in the hull roof suck air in. The troop compartment occupies the entire interior space behind the engine and gearbox. It can carry ten fully equipped soldiers; there are two seated in the middle of the hull, three looking outward on each side, and two more facing in the other direction.

Panhard M3 – Armoured Amphibious Personnel Carrier Specification	
Model	Panhard M3
Manufacturer	Panhard (French)
Country	Iraq
Year	1971–86
Engine	Panhard Model 4HD four-cylinder air-cooled petrol 90hp
Fuel	Petrol
Protection	Welded rolled steel (14mm)
Top Speed	56mph (90km/h)
Range	370 miles (595km)
Crew Capacity	Two, plus ten passengers
Length	15ft
Width	8ft
Height	7ft
Armament	Light small arms
Weight	6 tonnes
Service Branch	Iraqi Army

The M3's hull was made entirely of welded steel. Like the AML, the hull features a horizontal roofline, and a pointed tapering front. In order to deflect the blast of a land mine, the bottom of the hull construction is welded to a shallow V-shape. Located right behind the driver is the engine and gearbox. (US Army)

EE-11 Urutu

In the late 1980s, Iraqi military commanders were in need of more armoured protection for their infantry and opted to purchase the EE-11 Urutu. This was a Brazilian-manufactured amphibious armoured personnel carrier capable of carrying 11 soldiers. It came from the same line as the six-wheeled EE-9 Cascavel armoured reconnaissance vehicle and was also purchased from Brazil.

The Urutu was produced in numerous variants including a command platform, ambulance and recovery vehicle. In addition to having four emergency hatches in the hull roof, passengers can disembark from the vehicle through doors on each side, or the back. To provide soldiers with situational awareness, the troop compartment comes equipped as standard with fire ports and vision blocks. The hull is made of two separate layers of ballistic steel that are fused together and capable of withstanding small arms' fire at close range, including armour-piercing 7.62mm rounds.

A 12.7mm Browning M2 heavy machine gun was standard equipment on the Urutu. A gunner, located to the left of the driver in the hull, controls the machine gun. A stadia metric rangefinder and day/night sights with five-power magnification are also included at the gunner's station on all late production variants. Some Urutu variants used a single turret or pintle-mounted 7.62mm general purpose machine gun in place of the Browning heavy machine gun. It was also possible to mount heavier turrets with low-pressure cannons or gun-mortars for direct fire support, depending on the turret ring size. Later variants of the wheeled Urutu were powered by a six-cylinder, water-cooled engine and an automatic gearbox with five forward and one reverse gears.

EE-11 URUTU – Armoured Amphibious Personnel Carrier Specification	
Model	EE-11 Urutu
Manufacturer	Engesa (Brazil)
Country	Iraq
Year	1963
Engine	Detroit Diesel
Fuel	Diesel
Protection	Welded ballistic steel
Top Speed	55mph (88km/h)
Range	530 miles (852km)
Crew Capacity	Two, plus 11 passengers
Length	20ft
Width	9ft
Height	7ft
Armament	12.7mm M2 Browning machine gun
Weight	14 tonnes
Service Branch	Iraqi Army

In the late 1980s, Iraqi military commanders were in need of more armoured protection for their infantry and opted to purchase the EE-11 Urutu – a Brazilian-manufactured amphibious, armoured personnel carrier capable of carrying 11 soldiers. It came from the same line as the six-wheeled EE-9 Cascavel armoured reconnaissance vehicle, which was also purchased from Brazil in the 1980s. (US DoD)

Type 63 APC

The Type 63 armoured, tracked personnel carrier was a Chinese vehicle that was adopted by Iraq to expand its armoured capability. It was developed in the 1960s, and its low-profile design indicated that its designers had taken inspiration from the Soviet style. The Type 63 was an independent product of the People's Republic of China and Baghdad bought hundreds, which were used to ferry troops to the frontline. This ageing platform suffered from a lack of maintenance and achieved very little effectiveness on the battlefield. The '63' could carry 11 soldiers plus two crewmen. It was constructed from welded steel and offered protection from small arms' fire. The main access point for the embarked passengers was a rear opening, hinged door. While wheeled personnel carriers struggled in the sand with their weight ratio on their wheels, the tracked 63 was able to cope with most conditions. The driver's compartment had a single hatch cover that opened to the left, at the front of the hull. Two-day periscopes covering the left and right of the vehicle allowed the driver to navigate. A single hatch that opened to the right served as the commander's seat, and it was located on the front right of the hull. A 360-degree rotating periscope was also located on the upper surface of the commander hatch. A small hatch in the middle of the hull opened into the troop compartment, and in front of it was an open mount housing a machine gun with a calibre of 12.7mm. The main 12.7mm machine gun had 360-degree mount and a 90-degree elevation angle. In the 1991 Gulf War, dozens of 63s were attacked by Coalition fighter aircraft, crippling Saddam's ability to move his force before they faced an attack from the flank.

Type 63 – Armoured Personnel Carrier (Chinese) Specification	
Model	Type 63
Manufacturer	618 Factory, Norinco, China
Country	Iraq
Year	1963–90
Engine	8-cylinder air-cooled, turbo-charged diesel
Fuel	Diesel
Protection	Welded steel (14mm)
Top Speed	40mph (64km/h)
Range	310 miles (498km)
Crew Capacity	Two, plus ten passengers
Length	18ft
Width	10ft
Height	8ft
Armament	Type 54 12.7mm machine gun
Weight	13 tonnes
Service Branch	Iraqi Army

The Type 63 armoured tracked personnel carrier (APC) was a Chinese vehicle that entered service in the late 1960s. Its low-profile design suggests it carries the DNA of Soviet production, but the Type 63 was an independent product of the People's Republic of China. Baghdad bought hundreds of Type 63 APCs, which were used to ferry troops to the frontline. This ageing platform suffered from a lack of maintenance and achieved very little effectiveness on the battlefield. (US Army)

OT-62 TOPAS

The Topas armoured personnel carrier delivered heavy firepower, protection and mobility. The vehicle had been produced in a collaborative venture between Poland and Czechoslovakia. The front of the vehicle was angled, while the troop compartment was square – allowing room for up 16 soldiers. Access was through two rectangular roof hatches as well as hatches incorporated into the sides of the superstructure, but space was limited and potentially claustrophobic. Every crew member had access to an emergency hatch located beneath the driver's seat. The vehicle was equipped with three vision blocks, periscopes in a projecting bay, and a cupola with a vision block facing forward for the commander seated on the left side of the front. It opened forward, could be secured vertically, and was situated atop the projecting bay. Moreover, it featured two projecting bays rather than the one found in BTR-50 APCs, similar to the BTR-50PU command vehicle. The Iraqi version, designated OT-62A, was equipped with the Brazilian EE-9 Cascavel armoured car's slab-sided turret.

OT-62 TOPAS – Armoured Personnel Carrier Specification	
Model	OT-62 TOPAS
Manufacturer	Podpolianske Strojárne (PPS) plant Czechoslovak
Country	Iraq
Year	1962–2000
Engine	PV-6 6-cylinder, in line diesel 300hp
Fuel	Diesel
Protection	Welded rolled steel (17mm)
Top Speed	20mph (32km/h)
Range	200 miles (321km)
Crew Capacity	Two, plus 16 passengers
Length	23ft
Width	10ft
Height	7ft
Armament	14.5mm heavy machine gun in protected turret
Weight	13 tonnes
Service Branch	Iraqi Army

The Topas was a tracked armoured personnel carrier, which delivered heavy firepower, protection and mobility. It had a heavy calibre gun and, in addition to the driver and commander, could carry 16 passengers. The front of the vehicle was angled while the troop compartment was square. (US Army)

Walid

In the 1980s, Iraqi commanders sought to modernise some of their ageing armoured vehicles. The administration had borrowed millions of dollars from neighbouring Arab states and among the new procurements was the Walid armoured personnel carrier produced by Egypt. For better ballistic protection, the Walid's hull had sloping sides as opposed to the BTR-40's flat sides. Walid production proceeded with few changes to the original blueprint until 1981, when production engineers started to incorporate modified Mercedes Benz car parts. The vehicle is made up of an Egyptian-built armoured hull mounted on a German Magirus or Mercedes Benz truck chassis. The rear troop area was open topped with a canvas cover – some variants had hard covers. The hull features one door at the back of the hull and one on each side of the cab. Each side of the hull has three firing apertures as well. There was no night-vision system or NBC on the Walid.

Walid – Armoured Personnel Carrier Specification	
Model	Walid
Manufacturer	Kadar, Egypt (Based on BTR)
Country	Iraq
Year	1950–80s
Engine	Six-cylinder GAZ-40
Fuel	Petrol
Protection	Welded rolled steel (17mm)
Top Speed	60mph (96km/h)
Range	550 miles (885km)
Crew Capacity	Crew of two, plus 16 passengers
Length	20ft
Width	8ft
Height	8ft
Armament	7.62 gun in protected turret
Weight	10 tonnes
Service Branch	Iraqi Army

The Iraqi government purchased the Walid armoured personnel carrier from Egypt. The Walid's hull had sloping sides unlike the BTR-40's flat sides. The vehicle was made of an Egyptian-built armoured hull mounted on a German Magirus or Mercedes-Benz truck chassis. (US Army)

D-442 FUG

Iraq had added the D-442 FUG personnel carrier to its inventory in the 1970s. It was a small, amphibious armoured scout car and personnel carrier, which had been developed in Hungary. While listed as a personnel carrier, the FUG was small and carried just four 'scouts' or reconnaissance soldiers in addition to the crew. The FUG's main purpose was for reconnaissance and surveillance, a mobile command and observation post as well as an artillery observation post. The vehicle was powered by a four-cylinder, water-cooled diesel with a top speed of 55mph on surfaced roads and operational range of 280 miles. Its light armour was made of welded, homogeneous rolled steel and each plate was test-fired against an AK-47 under laboratory conditions. Although it had a much smaller appearance, the turret was very similar to that of OT-62B. There was little protection for the crew member who manned the 7.62mm light machine gun. The vehicle has traits in common with both BRDM-1 and BRDM-2, but it lacked a permanent armament. The FUG played a limited role in the Gulf War; some were seen on the Mutla ridge when Coalition forces attacked Iraqi forces fleeing Kuwait.

D-442 FUG – Armoured Personnel Car Specification	
Model	D-442 FUG (Hungary)
Manufacturer	Danube Shipyard
Country	Iraq
Year	1964–present
Engine	Csepel D414.44 in-line 4-cylinder OHV 5.5-litre diesel 101hp
Diesel	Diesel
Protection	Welded rolled steel (13mm)
Top Speed	55mph (88km/h)
Range	350 miles (563km)
Crew Capacity	Three, plus four scouts
Length	19ft
Width	8ft
Height	6ft
Armament	7.62mm gun in protected turret (D-442 DUG)
Weight	6 tonnes
Service Branch	Iraqi Army

The D-442 Fug was a small, wheeled reconnaissance vehicle, which had been developed in Hungary. The FUG's main purpose was to provide intelligence, reconnaissance and surveillance. It also acted as a mobile command and observation post and an artillery observation post. (US Army)

MT-LB Tracked Armoured Vehicle

The huge Iraqi Army included several hundred Soviet-produced MT-LB amphibious, tracked armoured fighting vehicles in 1991. In production since the 1970s, the MT-LB presented a low-profile with a 12.7mm heavy machine gun and protected cupola on the top of the chassis. The driver and the commander/gunner, who make up the crew, are seated in a compartment at the front of the car, with the engine situated behind them. The vehicle can carry up to 11 troops or 4,00lb of equipment in a compartment in the back. Its light armour allows the MT-LB to deliver a speed of 45mph. Propelled by a V-8 diesel engine, the MT-LB was upgraded by the Iraqis with the addition of a ZU-23 anti-aircraft gun, which was positioned in an open-top turret. MT-LBs were deployed in the desert but failed to make any real impact, with most being engaged by Coalition forces.

MT-LB – Armoured Personnel Car Specification	
Model	MT-LB Ukraine
Manufacturer	Kharkiv Tractor Centre, Ukraine
Country	Iraq
Year	1970s
Engine	YaMZ 238 V8 diesel
Diesel	Diesel
Protection	Welded rolled steel (14mm)
Top Speed	38mph (61km/h)
Range	310 miles (498km)
Crew Capacity	Two, plus 11 passengers
Length	21ft
Width	10ft
Height	6ft
Armament	12.7mm NSV/Kord heavy machine gun
Weight	12 tonnes
Service Branch	Iraqi Army

Above left: In 1991, the huge Iraqi Army included in its weaponry several hundred Soviet-produced MT-LB amphibious, tracked armoured fighting vehicles. In production since the 1970s, the MT-LB presented a low-profile with a 12.7mm heavy machine gun and protected cupola on the top of the chassis. (US Army)

Above right: This image shows an Iraqi MT-LB converted into a self propelled anti-aircraft gun armed with a ZU-2 anti-aircraft gun. The driver and the commander/gunner, who make up the crew, are seated in a compartment at the front of the car, with the engine situated behind them. The vehicle can carry up to 11 troops or 4,000lb of equipment in a compartment in the back. (US Army)

MOWAG Roland

The MOWAG Roland was a Swiss-made armoured personnel carrier, which was procured to support Iraq's mechanised infantry. Like many of Baghdad's military investments, it came with little service support or spares. Commanders struggled to find a role for this small four-wheel drive vehicle, which operated with a crew of three and had space for three troops. It was regarded as too small to ferry a platoon and not suitable for reconnaissance tasks. Officially variants included use as a rocket launcher, armoured troop carrier and ambulance.

In reality, the Rowland saw little service. Access points are positioned to allow the occupants to enter and exit from the left, right, and the rear. The Roland had three daylight periscopes fitted, which were located in the front. For night-time driving, the centre one could be changed for a passive periscope. The turret above the gunner's position could be manually rotated 360 degrees. A day-vision block and a single-piece hatch cover that opens to the rear are present. In addition, air conditioning, passive night vision, searchlights, and an obstacle-clearing blade were mounted at the front of the hull. MOWAG incorporated firing ports that allowed the troops to aim and fire their weapons from within the vehicle safely – very similar to the Soviet style of design. The MOWAG's tyres were bulletproof with metal discs on each side of the tyre that supported a punctured tyre and added traction when travelling over rough terrain.

MOWAG Roland – Armoured Personnel Car Specification	
Model	Mowag Roland
Manufacturer	Mowag, Switzerland
Country	Iraq
Year	1964–80
Engine	V 8 Chrysler LA 318-3 160hp
Diesel	Diesel
Protection	Welded rolled steel (14mm)
Top Speed	62mph (99km/h)
Range	200 miles (321km)
Crew Capacity	Two, plus four PAX
Length	16ft
Width	7ft
Height	6ft
Armament	Light support section weapons mounted from turret
Weight	4 tonnes
Service Branch	Iraqi Army

The MOWAG Roland was a Swiss-made armoured personnel carrier, which was procured to support Iraq's mechanised infantry. It was a robust platform equipped with four-wheel drive. This small APC operated with a crew of three with additional space for three troops and was regarded as too small to ferry a platoon and not suitable for reconnaissance tasks. (US Army)

BTR-50

Built on the PT-76 light tank chassis, the BTR-50 was a Soviet-tracked amphibious armoured personnel carrier (APC) with the nickname the 'armoured transporter'. It entered service with the Iraqi Army in the late 1970s with Baghdad procuring 150 vehicles. The BTR-50 was first produced by the Soviet Army in 1954 and was upgraded several times to ensure it could maintain the same speed as Moscow's main battle tanks. Despite not having any dedicated weapons, it remained in service for decades with the Soviet armed forces and later the Iraqis. The driver operated the BTR-50 with two tillers to turn left and right, with a floor plate for acceleration and braking. When closed down, the driver relied on three vision blocks, which like all 'assisted viewing windows' required significant training to manage. The crew compartment was directly behind the driver's seat and was very small. Numerous variants were developed and procured by the Iraqis. Saddam's commanders procured a range of these vintage Soviet armoured vehicles, but yet again their maintenance resources were limited. The crew compartment was located in front, the troop compartment was in the middle, and the engine compartment at the back. Up to 20 fully outfitted infantrymen could be transported in it, sitting on benches spanning the entire troop compartment.

BTR-50 – Armoured Personnel Carrier (Tracked) Specification	
Model	BTR-50 Armoured Personnel Carrier (amphibious capability)
Manufacturer	Soviet government factories
Country	Iraq
Year	1954–70s
Engine	V-6 6-cylinder 4-stroke in line water-cooled diesel
Diesel	Diesel
Protection	Homogenous welded steel (13mm at the front)
Top Speed	30mph (48km/h)
Range	250 miles (402km)
Crew Capacity	Two, plus 20 passengers
Length	23ft
Width	10ft
Height	7ft
Armament	Light support section weapons mounted from turret
Weight	14 tonnes
Service Branch	Iraqi Army

The BTR 50 was a Soviet-tracked amphibious APC with the nickname the 'armoured transporter'. It entered service with the Iraqi Army in the late 1970s when defence ministers in Baghdad procured 150 vehicles. The driver operated the BTR-50 with two tillers to turn left and right, and a floor plate for acceleration and braking. (US Army)

When closed down, the driver relied on three vision blocks on the BTR-50, which like all 'assisted viewing windows' required significant training to manage. (US Army)

BTR-60

The BTR-60 was the first in a line of a new-generation Soviet APCs. It was an eight wheeled 'drive' vehicle with a long hull with angled sides, which included an armoured roof and a protected hull made from a welded steel construction. Its design followed the adopted concept of driver and commander seated at the front, a personnel compartment in the mid-section, and the engine compartment at the rear of the hull.

The BTR-60 could carry 14 soldiers and its flat roof was often used as a platform for additional troops – although they had no armoured protection. Inside the troop compartment, three firing ports were located on each side to allow soldiers to fire from a protected position. Despite the size of the BTR-60, the driver had little room or vision. It was very difficult to see to the left or right and extensive training was needed to drive the vehicle. A coaxial 14.5mm KPV heavy machine gun and a 7.62mm PKT machine gun could be fitted to the BTR-60 to the right, with a telescopic sight mounted coaxially on the left. Earlier versions of the vehicle had an open troop compartment, which left it vulnerable to attack. The BTR-60 sat high off the ground and two steps were fitted on each side of the hull, one between the first and second set of road wheels and the other between the third and fourth set, to aid the infantry in mounting and dismounting the vehicle. It was powered by two six-cylinder petrol engines, positioned side by side and situated at the back of the vehicle. Each engine powered two wheels in the vehicle. The first and third axles were propelled by the engine on the left, while the second and fourth axles were propelled by the engine on the right. The two-engine design was seen as revolutionary – although expensive. It had the advantage that each engine could work without the other. This meant that if one engine was disabled, it did not affect the other one and the vehicle could still move, albeit with reduced speed.

The BTR-60 was completely amphibious, using a jet positioned in the centre of the back of the hull to push it through the water but it was prone to malfunctions. The BTR-60 was a Soviet workhorse and was used to ferry Iraqi soldiers into Kuwait.

BTR-60 – Armoured Personnel Carrier (Wheeled) Specification	
Model	BTR-60 armoured personnel carrier (wheeled)
Manufacturer	Soviet government factories. V A Dedkov
Country	Iraq
Year	1959–present
Engine	2 GAZ-40 p V-6 6-cylinder petrol
Diesel	Petrol
Protection	Homogenous welded steel 5–10mm
Top Speed	50mph (80km/h)
Range	300 miles (482km)
Crew Capacity	Three, plus 14 passengers
Length	22ft
Width	9ft
Height	8ft
Armament	14.5mm KPVT heavy machine gun plus 7.62mm coaxial machine gun
Weight	10 tonnes
Service Branch	Iraqi Army

The eight-wheeled Soviet-armoured personnel carriers were the first of a new generation of vehicles. The two-engine design was seen as revolutionary – although expensive. It had the advantage that each engine could work without the other. (US Army)

The driver and commander sat at the front alongside each other. The BTR-60 could carry 14 soldiers and its flat roof was often used as a platform for additional troops. (US Army)

BTR-80

The BTR-80 was introduced in 1986 as a heavily upgraded and modern variant of the original vehicle. It operates a single V-8 turbocharged water-cooled diesel engine – delivering more power than the twin petrol engines seen in the BTR-60. The BTR-80's armament includes a 14.5mm KPVT heavy machine gun and 7.62mm PKT (PKTM) machine gun. The crew can enter and leave the vehicle through the upper hatches in the hull roof or the side doors – the latter enable the crew to enter and exit even when the vehicle is on the move. The BTR-80 delivers high mobility with its eight-wheel running gear and all-wheel drive, the powerful diesel engine, an independent wishbone torsion-bar suspension and bulletproof tubeless tyres. The vehicle is capable of crossing water obstacles without preparation. The hull and turret armour are able to protect the crew from small arms fire but is vulnerable to anti-tank missiles. The BTR-80 operates a crew of three—comprising a driver, commander, and gunner—and accommodates up to seven fully equipped soldiers. The BTR-80 family of combat and logistic support vehicles has been developed and built around the BTR-80 chassis: a battalion commander APC, nuclear and chemical reconnaissance vehicle, a variety of communications, control and command staff vehicles, an armoured medical vehicle, an armoured recovery vehicle and the 120mm Nona-SVK self-propelled artillery gun.

BTR – 80 - Armoured Personnel Carrier (Wheeled) Specification	
Model	BTR-80 armoured personnel carrier (wheeled)
Manufacturer	Arzamas Machine Building Plant
Country	Iraq
Year	1984–present
Engine	Diesel Kam AZ-7403 260hp
Diesel	Diesel
Protection	Armour (10mm at front)
Top Speed	50mph (80km/h)
Range	370 miles (595km)
Crew Capacity	Three, plus seven passengers
Length	25ft
Width	9ft
Height	8ft
Armament	14.5mm KPVT heavy machine gun and one 30mm 2A72
Weight	14 tonnes
Service Branch	Iraqi Army

In 1986, the BTR-80 was introduced and Iraq quickly purchased a number of them. It used a single V-8 turbocharged water-cooled diesel engine – delivering more power than the twin petrol engines seen in the BTR-60. The BTR-80's armament includes a 14.5mm KPVT heavy machine gun and 7.62mm PKT (PKTM) machine gun. (US Army)

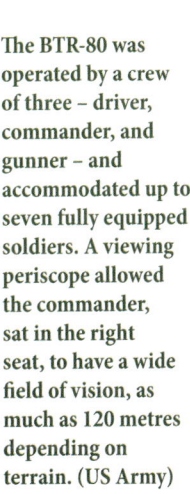

The BTR-80 was operated by a crew of three – driver, commander, and gunner – and accommodated up to seven fully equipped soldiers. A viewing periscope allowed the commander, sat in the right seat, to have a wide field of vision, as much as 120 metres depending on terrain. (US Army)

OT M-60

The OTM-60 was an armoured personnel carrier developed by Yugoslavia in the early 1960s. It had a similar profile to the US M113 and the British 432 APCs. It was the first Yugoslav armoured vehicle to enter mass production. Research and development began in 1956, and the first prototype was produced in June 1958. Prior to the commencement of full production in 1962, the armoured carrier was known as Objekat M-590. Iraq purchased 190 M-60s, which were used in the troop-carrying role, as well as a command platform, ambulance, and anti-tank variant. The vehicle was powered by a six-cylinder diesel engine, which generates 140hp, giving a top road speed of 45km/h. The vehicle was an all-welded steel construction, which gave protection against small arms. It had no NBC protection system. Operated by a crew of three, the vehicle was equipped with armour to counter small arms fire and was fitted with a 12.7mm M2 HB Browning heavy machine gun, as well as a coaxial 7.92 M53 machine-gun with a capacity of 2,000 rounds. Powered by a Famos FFTR six-cylinder engine, the OTM M60 could reach speeds of 28mph.

OTM-60 – Armoured Personnel Carrier (Tracked) Specification	
Model	OTM-60 armoured personnel carrier
Manufacturer	Military Technical Institute (Yugoslavia)
Country	Iraq
Year	1956–no longer in service
Engine	Famos FFTR 150hp
Diesel	Diesel
Protection	Armour 10–25mm
Top Speed	28mph (45km/h)
Range	250 miles (402km)
Crew Capacity	Three
Length	16ft
Width	9ft
Height	6ft
Armament	12.7mm Browning heavy machine gun – coaxial 7.92mm M53 machine gun
Weight	11 tonnes
Service Branch	Iraqi Army

The OTM-60 was an armoured personnel carrier developed by Yugoslavia in the early 1960s. It had a similar profile to the US M113 and the British 432 armoured personnel carriers. The OTM-60 was the first Yugoslav armoured vehicle to enter serial production. Research and development had begun in 1956, and the first prototype was produced in June 1958. (US Army)

Panhard VCR

The French six-wheeled (and four-wheeled) Panhard VCR armoured vehicle was purchased by Iraq in 1981 with a total of 100 put into service. The engine was located in the front right, with the driver's seat positioned over the front wheels. Those who drove the VCR described the driver's view as being much improved, but drivers spoke of suffering travel sickness when they drove the vehicle with hatches closed. All sides of the VCR were protected by steel armour to counter small arms fire. It was fitted with a 12.7mm heavy machine gun or a 7.62mm light machine gun deployed on a ring mount on the left of the roof. Iraq purchased the VCR in the anti-tank role, which was called the Tourelle and known as the VCR/TH. It was fitted with wire-guided ATGMs. Few VCRs were seen in 1991, with the majority believed to have been kept in reserve for defence against Coalition forces if they had advanced to Baghdad.

Panhard VCR – Armoured Personnel Carrier (six wheeled) Specification	
Model	Panhard VCR armoured personnel carrier
Manufacturer	Panhard (France)
Country	Iraq
Year	1979–2000
Engine	Peugeot PRV V-6 145hp
Diesel	Diesel
Protection	Armour 12mm
Top Speed	60mph (96km/h)
Range	430 miles (692km)
Crew Capacity	Three, plus nine passengers
Length	16ft
Width	8ft
Height	7ft
Armament	12.7mm Browning heavy machine gun – HOT missile system
Weight	8 tonnes
Service Branch	Iraqi Army

The French six-wheeled (and four-wheeled) Panhard VCR armoured vehicle was purchased by Iraq in 1981 with a total of 100 put into service. The engine is located in the front, to the right, with the driver's seat positioned over the front wheels. Those who drove the VCR described the driver's view as being much better than that in other vehicles. (French Armed Forces)

Chapter 5
The Gulf States

Kuwait | Egypt | Saudi Arabia | Syria

The invasion of Kuwait in August 1990 by Saddam Hussein's forces ignited a collective response from the international community and most of the Gulf States, who called on Baghdad to withdraw its forces. The United Nations Security Council declared on 2 August, the day of the invasion, that the Iraqi action of ignoring the basic order of the international community was a violation of international law and adopted Resolution 660, which required the immediate and unconditional withdrawal of Iraqi forces. Saddam ignored the UN and a Coalition headed by Saudi Arabia, Egypt, Bahrain, Qatar, Syria as well as exiled Kuwaiti forces was quickly formed. It was headed by the US and supported by the UK and many Western nations.

The wider Coalition members included Argentina, Australia, Bahrain, Bangladesh, Belgium, Canada, Czechoslovakia, Denmark, Egypt, France, Germany, Greece, Honduras, Hungary, Italy, Japan, Kuwait, Luxembourg, Morocco, the Netherlands, New Zealand, Niger, Norway, Oman, Pakistan, the Philippines, Poland, Portugal, Qatar, Romania, Saudi Arabia, Senegal, Sierra Leone, Singapore, South Korea, Spain, Sweden, Syria, Turkey, the United Arab Emirates, the United Kingdom and the United States. Germany and Japan provided financial assistance and donated military hardware, although they did not send direct military assistance. This policy was later dubbed 'chequebook diplomacy'. Although Russia did not commit troops, it joined the United States in condemning Iraq, its long-time client state.

The Kuwaiti Army in exile consisted of four brigades, totalling 12,000 men, equipped with more than 140 Chieftain and M-84 tanks. The principal armoured unit was the 38th Kuwaiti Armoured Brigade, dubbed the 'Al Shadid' or Martyrs. It had lost 22 of its Chieftains during the Iraqi assault into Kuwait. The 35th Kuwaiti Mechanised Brigade was equipped with M113 tracked armoured personnel carriers. The biggest Arab contingent came from Egypt and included the 3rd Mechanized Division, which deployed 200 M60 main battle tanks and 300 M113 armoured personnel carriers, while the 4th Armoured Division arrived with 250 M60s and 250 M113s.

Syria committed 19,000 men, consisting of one airborne brigade and the 9th Armoured Division, which was equipped with more than 200 T-62 tanks. In return for its support, Syria received US$1 billion from Saudi Arabia. Both Egypt and Syria stated that their troops were only to be deployed to defend Saudi Arabia, though this approach was to change. Saudi Arabia contributed Saudi Arabian Armed Forces, and the country's reserve, the Saudi Arabian National Guard. The Royal Saudi Land Forces fielded 40,000 soldiers, organised into two armoured brigades, four mechanised brigades, one infantry and one airborne brigade. The Saudi force included the 8th, 10th, 11th and 20th mechanised brigades equipped with 550 French AMX-30s and US M60 tanks. Qatar also provided an armoured battalion equipped with about 24 French-supplied AMX-30 tanks, while Bahrain sent a brigade supported with M60A main battle tanks.

The Sultan of Oman sent a battalion of infantry and a small number of Scimitar armoured reconnaissance vehicles. The United Arab Emirates also deployed infantry troops as part of the Gulf Co-operation Council and the Operation *Peninsula Shield* force that advanced into the city of Kuwait. In total, the Coalition gathered half a million men from 42 countries armed with 3,400 tanks and an estimated 9,000 armoured vehicles.

A number of resolutions were voted by the Arab League and UN Security Council in reference to Iraq's invasion of Kuwait. Resolution 678 was passed on 29 November 1990; it authorised 'all necessary means to uphold and implement Resolution 660', as well as the use of force diplomatically in the event that Iraq would not comply. It also gave Iraq until 15 January 1991 to depart. The war consisted of two phases: the first was codenamed Operation *Desert Shield* (2 August 1990–17 January 1991) for operations leading to the build-up of troops and defence of Saudi Arabia. The second was Operation *Desert Storm* (17 January–28 February 1991), the combat phase, with the initial conflict in January being air strikes. The co-operation among these states underscored their commitment to regional stability and their resolve to defend against external threats. Their strategic alliance demonstrated unity among the Gulf nations and solidified broader international efforts, notably under the leadership of the United States, to confront Iraq and liberate Kuwait. The formation of this coalition marked a pivotal moment in the history of the Gulf region, showcasing the strength of collective action in the face of tyranny and aggression.

Kuwait

The M-84 – Main Battle Tank

The M-84 was a variant of the the Soviet T-72, which was produced in Yugoslavia and incorporated many improvements, including a domestic fire-control system that the T-72M lacked, improved composite armour, and a larger engine. In the late 1970s, following extensive and challenging negotiations with the Soviet Union, Yugoslavia successfully obtained a licence for the production of T-72M tanks. As a licensed copy, the M-84 maintained the same armour protection as the T-72M. The frontal hull armour consisted of a 3in rolled homogeneous armour (RHA) steel plate, followed by 4in of glass-reinforced plastic called textolite, backed by a thin steel plate. This armour arrangement gave the tank protection against High Explosive Anti-Tank (HEAT) projectiles. The M-84 was powered by the V-46TK diesel engine, rated at 780hp, providing the tank with a top road speed of 6km/h. While the designs of the M-84 and the T-72M were notably similar, the M-84 was distinguished by incorporating a superior domestic fire-control system, replacing the notoriously downgraded fire-control system in the T-72M tanks. The M-84 had entered service with the Yugoslav People's Army in 1984 and was purchased by Kuwait in 1989. It was armed with a 125mm smoothbore cannon derived from the Soviet 2A46 barrel. The tank's fume extractor was positioned in the middle of the barrel and was shielded with a thermal coating that minimised deformation of the barrel from high temperatures and ensured it cooled at the same rate during rapid firing. The M-84 used an automatic loader, which enabled it to sustain a firing rate of eight rounds per minute. Ammunition (40 rounds) were stowed in the hull of the tank beneath the turret, which proved to be a weakness. While the lower hull beneath the turret, where the ammunition was kept, was one of the least likely places to be hit and penetrated by anti-tank rounds or mines, it was a deadly location if it was penetrated followed by secondary detonation of the ammunition, meaning the crew and tank were unlikely to survive the explosion.

Left: The M-84 was a variant of the Soviet T-72, which was produced in Yugoslavia and incorporated many improvements, including a domestic fire-control system that the T-72M lacked, improved composite armour, and a larger engine. (DPL)

Below left: A Kuwaiti M-84 tank crosses a trench during preparations for war in the desert. The 41-tonne tank has a crew of three and could reach speeds of 42mph. (DPL)

Below right: The M-84 uses an automatic loader, which enables it to sustain a firing rate of eight rounds per minute. Ammunition (40 rounds) was stowed in the hull of the tank beneath the turret, which proved to be a weakness. (US Army)

M-84 – Main Battle Tank Specification	
Model	M-84
Manufacturer	Military Technical Institute	Euro Eakovic (Croatia)
Country	Former Yugoslavia
Year	1979–83
Engine	Diesel V-46TK 1,000hp (750kW)
Fuel	Diesel
Protection	Composite alloy; including high-hardness steel, glass-reinforced plastic, RHA steel, and either sand or granite
Top Speed	42mph (67km/h)
Range	450 miles (724km)
Crew Capacity	Three
Length	23ft
Width	12ft
Height	7ft
Armament	L11A5 125mm rifled gun, 2A46 smoothbore gun
Weight	41 tonnes
Service Branch	Kuwait

Right: The M-84 was armed with a 125mm smoothbore gun, fitted with an autoloader. This MBT is complete with Yugoslavian fire control system. The M-84 also carried extra fuel drums at the rear of the tank. (US Army)

Below left: Many M-84 tank crews and their vehicles escaped the Iraqi advance and trained with Coalition forces prior to the operation in February 1991. At the end of the war, they headed a victory parade through Kuwait. (US Army)

Below right: The Yugoslav M-84 resembles the T-72 only in outward appearance. There are minor differences in the external features of the turret, with a bank of six electrically operated 81mm smoke grenade dischargers at each side of the turret and a meteorology sensor pole on the forward part of the turret. (US DoD)

FV4201 Chieftain Main Battle Tank

The Chieftain tank had been selected by Kuwait in 1989 to serve a key role in its frontline armoured formations. A development of the Centurion, the FV4201 was heavily armoured. The new design introduced the reclining driver position, which initially was found to be difficult. Its inclusion allowed the platform to incorporate a heavily sloped hull and reduced the height of the tank. A new powerpack and improved transmission gave it higher speed than the Centurion despite being heavier due to major upgrades to armour protection. Prior to the Iraqi invasion, Kuwait's armoured holdings included 70 old British Vickers Mk1 tanks, and 40 Centurions. Both were in the process of being withdrawn from service and being replaced with 165 Chieftain MBTs and a smaller number of Yugoslavian-built M-84s. By August 1990, only a small number of M-84s had been delivered. In addition, more than 200 Soviet T-72s built under licence, were still on order but not delivered.

Despite months of Iraqi sabre-rattling, Kuwait did not have its forces on alert and was caught unaware when Iraq struck. Kuwaiti forces resisted but were vastly outnumbered. In central Kuwait, the 35th Armoured Brigade fought a delaying action near Al Jahra , west of Kuwait City. In the south, the 15th Armoured Brigade moved immediately to evacuate its forces to Saudi Arabia.

In the late 1980s, Kuwait purchased 165 Chieftain MBTs and a smaller number of Yugoslavian-built M-84s to upgrade its armoured divisions – with the Chieftain replacing the older Centurion. By August 1990, only a small number of M-84s had been delivered. In addition, more than 200 Soviet T-72s built under licence, were on order but not delivered. (DPL)

The Chieftain tank had been selected by Kuwait in 1989 to serve a key role in its frontline armoured formations. A development of the Centurion, the FV4201 was heavily armoured and was deployed with the 15th Armoured Brigade. (US Army)

Chieftain (FV 4201) Main Battle Tank Specification	
Model	Chieftain
Manufacturer	Leyland Motors
Country	United Kingdom
Year	1960s–90s
Engine	Leyland L60 multi-fuel two-stroke opposed piston compression ignition. 750hp
Fuel	Diesel
Protection	Glacis: 127mm
Top Speed	25mph (40km/h)
Range	310 miles (498km)
Crew Capacity	Four
Length	35ft
Width	12ft
Height	10ft
Armament	L11A5 120mm-rifled gun
Weight	55 tonnes
Service Branch	Kuwait

BMP-2 – Infantry Fighting Vehicle

The BMP-2 is an armoured personnel carrier designed and operated by Soviet and Eastern Block forces. Kuwait purchased 118, which were delivered between 1995 and 1996. The BMP-2 has a crew of three and the capability to ferry seven soldiers. It is fitted with a 30mm gun and with a maximum

Above left: The Kuwaiti armed forces procured the BMP-armoured personnel carrier, which had been designed and operated by Soviet and Eastern Block forces. Kuwait purchased 118, which were delivered between 1995 and 1996. It was deployed with a crew of three and had the capability to ferry seven soldiers. (DPL)

Above right: Kuwaiti soldiers are pictured eating near their BMP on open ground near the British Embassy after the conflict. The BMP appears to have an anti-tank rocket system fixed to the top of the cupola. (US Army)

speed of 45mph was one of the fastest armoured platforms available in the late 1990s. The BMP has an unconventional layout. The driver of the BMP-2 sits in the front left of the vehicle, with the engine in a separate compartment to his right. The six-cylinder Model UTD-20 supercharged diesel engine can develop 285/300hp at 2,600rpm. There are three stations: one for the driver in the middle and two for the machine-gunners on both sides of the driver's seat. The fighting compartment is arranged in the middle of the hull where the stations for a commander and gunner are located.

BMP-2 – Armoured Infantry Fighting Vehicle Specification	
Model	BMP-2 – Infantry Fighting Vehicle
Manufacturer	Kurganmashzavod
Country	Soviet Union
Year	1980–present
Engine	Diesel UTD-20/3. 300hp
Diesel	Diesel
Protection	Steel armour 33mm
Top Speed	45mph (72km/h)
Range	370 miles (595km)
Crew Capacity	Three, plus seven passengers
Length	22ft
Width	10ft
Height	8ft
Armament	30mm 2A42 autocannon, 9M113 Konkurs ATGM
Weight	15 tonnes
Service Branch	Kuwaiti Army

Kuwaiti soldiers celebrate victory at the end of the war. The BMP 3 had a crew of three and the capability to ferry seven soldiers. It was fitted with a 30mm gun and with a maximum speed of 45mph was one of the fastest armoured platforms available in the late 1990s. (David Reynolds/DPL)

M113 – Armoured Personnel Carrier

Kuwait purchased several hundred US Army M113s in the late 1980s. The M113 has been used as a troop carrier and command platform and when Iraqi forces invaded, Kuwait's small standing army had little chance to deploy its armoured forces. Those units with M113s, which escaped the Iraqi invasion, joined UK forces in the desert and then spearheaded the advance back into Kuwait. The M113 is an incredibly versatile platform, which still remains in service with the United States and many other countries. The M113 is a tracked APC that was developed for the United States Army in the early 1960s. The vehicle is powered by a reliable and durable Detroit Diesel 6V53T diesel engine. This provides good mobility, both on and off-road, and it is relatively easy to maintain. The M113 is also equipped with a number of features that provide the occupants with protection from small arms fire and shrapnel. It can ferry 11 fully-equipped soldiers. The vehicle's armour is made of aluminium alloy, which provides a good balance between weight and protection. The vehicle is also equipped with vision ports and periscopes, which provide the occupants with a good field of view.

Kuwaitis and British troops exercise in the desert in early 1991. The M113 APC was designed by FMC. The main design features of the vehicle included fully enclosed armour made with aircraft-quality aluminium alloy. Most of the components of the vehicle were made of light alloys. (DPL)

A Kuwaiti M113 APC drives into the city at the end of the war. Kuwait purchased several hundred US Army M113s in the late 1980s. The M113 was also used as a command platform. (David Reynolds/DPL)

M113 – Armoured Personnel Carrier Specification	
Model	Armoured Personnel Carrier
Manufacturer	General Motors | General Dynamics Land Systems
Country	United States/Canada
Year	1960–present
Engine	Detroit diesel
Fuel	Diesel
Protection	5083 aluminium alloy 28–44mm
Top Speed	42mph on surface road (67km/h), 3mph in water (4km/h)
Range	300 miles (480km)
Crew Capacity	Two crew, commander, driver, plus 11–15 passengers
Length	15ft
Width	9ft
Height	8ft
Armament	M2 Browning machine gun
Weight	12 tonnes

Egypt

The M-60 Main Battle Tank

The Egyptian Army had procured hundreds of M-60 tanks from the United States in the late 1980s, and the government in Cairo was one of the first Arab nations to step forward and offer support to Kuwait when Iraq invaded. Egypt sent more than 35,000 troops and several hundred tanks to

Above left: The Egyptian Army had procured hundreds of M60 tanks from the United States in the 1980s, and the Cairo government was one of the first Arab nations to step forward and offer military assistance to defend Kuwait. (US Army)

Above right: The US Army trained and supported the Egyptian military with the development of its M60 tanks. They were issued to the two independent tank brigades and then to the 4th and 9th Armoured Divisions. (US Army)

Saudi Arabia in support of Operation *Desert Storm*. It was the second largest contingent, after the US, and the key Arab partner in the 42-nation coalition against Iraq. Egyptian M-60 tanks joined Kuwaiti forces to spearhead the coalition ground offensive against Iraq. The procurement of the M-60 came in 1988 when the government approved the purchase of 700 M60A1s. Egypt routinely operated alongside US and UK forces on war games in the Egyptian desert and the arms agreement included US Army personnel training and supporting the Egyptian military with the development of the M-60 tank force. The M-60 was issued first to the two independent tank brigades and then to the 4th and 9th Armoured Divisions. Outside the US, the Egyptian Army had one of the biggest M-60 forces. The tanks were loaded aboard ships and ferried to Saudi Arabia. During the Coalition advance, the Egyptian armoured force played a key role and was among the first to enter Kuwait.

M-60 – Main Battle Tank Specification	
Model	M-60 | upgraded M60-A1 | M60-A2 | M60-A3
Manufacturer	Chrysler Corporation Delaware Defence Plant
Country	United States
Year	1960, subsequently upgraded in 1962, 1974 and 1979
Engine	Continental AVDS-1790 series turbo supercharged, fuel injection, 12-cylinder, 750hp (559kW)
Fuel	Diesel
Protection	Cast homogeneous armour steel hull and turret with Kevlar lining
Top Speed	30mph (48km/h)
Range	310 miles (498km)
Crew Capacity	Four
Length	30ft
Width	12ft
Height	10ft
Armament	105mm M68 rifled gun, 7.62mm machine guns and .50 cal M85 heavy machine guns.
Weight	50 tonnes
Service Branch	Egyptian Army

M113 – Armoured Personnel Carrier

The Egyptian military purchased more than 1,500 former US Army M113s in the late 1980s. In 1990, the Egyptian military had more than 400,000 personnel and maintained a close working relationship with Washington. This co-operation eased integration of the Egyptian Army in the Gulf War coalition of 1990–91. The Egyptian II Corps, under Major General Salah Halabi, with the 3rd Mechanised Division and 4th Armoured Division, fought as part of the Arab Joint Forces Command North. The deployed force came under heavy Iraqi fire and struggled to secure its first objective. While the Egyptians were well armed, their poor communication caused confusion. They were unable to re-group and were late to join the ceremonial drive into Kuwait by Arab armour.

M113 – Armoured Personnel Carrier Specification

Model	Armoured personnel carrier
Manufacturer	General Motors | General Dynamics Land Systems
Country	United States/Canada
Year	1960–present
Engine	Detroit Diesel
Fuel	Diesel
Protection	5083 aluminium alloy 28–44mm
Top Speed	42mph on surface road (67km/h), 3mph in water (4km/h)
Range	300 miles (480km)
Crew Capacity	Two crew, commander, driver, plus 11–15 passengers
Length	16ft
Width	9ft
Height	8ft
Armament	M2 Browning machine gun
Weight	12 tonnes
Service Branch	Egyptian Army

Above left: The Egyptian military purchased more than 1,500 former US Army M113s in the late 1980s. The armoured personnel carriers could carry eight to ten soldiers, with the driver sat at the front left and the commander in the middle of the tracked platform. (DPL)

Above right: The Egyptian Army fitted heavy machine guns to its M113 in the Gulf conflict. Additional ammunition was carried alongside the commander's seat. All three M113s in this image, taken in the Saudi desert in October 1990, show the vehicles carrying camouflage netting on the roof behind the gunner. (DPL)

The Egyptian armed forces were well armed and trained, having taken part in annual exercises with the US in Egypt called Exercise 'Bright Star'. (US Army)

Pegaso BMR 600

When they deployed to the Gulf, the Egyptian Marines took the innovative amphibious Pegaso armoured personnel vehicle with them. Cairo had purchased 250 from Spain in the 1980s. The six-wheeled vehicle could ferry ten fully equipped soldiers and had a crew of two. It was fast, well protected, but had little fire power with one single 7.62mm MG 42 machine gun. In the earlier 1980s, a protected cupola was fitted to the right side of the vehicle. It had eight vision devices around it and an additional one at the front top. The Egyptian Army order comprised 217 vehicles in the APC role, 13 command post vehicles, 10 recovery and maintenance vehicles and 10 ambulances. The engine was positioned vertically towards the front left, behind the driver's position and the engine's exhaust ran all the way to the rear on the left-hand side. Inside there was room for infantry soldiers and racks on each side, which allowed additional equipment to be carried. The rear ramp dropped vertically and was powered by a hydraulic lift. The Pegaso 3500 was designed with amphibious capabilities in mind. At the front of the vehicle there was a trim vane. Hydrojets were installed at the rear, on each side of the access ramp. During operations in the Gulf, the Pegaso performed well and was the main vehicle of the country's marines for many years. In service, Egyptian commanders designated the Pegaso as the BMR 300.

Egypt expected to take part in an amphibious assault into Kuwait and carried out numerous exercises, including with the British. The innovative amphibious Pegaso, armoured personnel vehicle, was primarily used to carry troops, but was also deployed in medical and command variants. (DPL)

The six-wheeled Pegaso was seen as a revolution in armoured personnel carriers. It had an automatic gearbox; it could be driven across difficult and hilly terrain and was amphibious. A heavy machine gun appears to have been fitted to the rear of these vehicles. Despite its armoured protection and off-road capability, the Egyptians quickly discovered that tracks work better in the sand. (DPL)

Pegaso BMR 300 – Wheeled Amphibious Armoured Personnel Carrier Specification	
Model	Tracked Cargo Carrier
Manufacturer	Enasa
Country	Spain
Year	1970
Engine	Pegaso 9156/8, 352hp
Fuel	Diesel
Protection	Reinforced armoured aluminium, which could withstand 14.5mm rounds
Top Speed	49mph (78km/h)
Range	360 miles (579km)
Crew Capacity	Nine
Length	21ft
Width	9ft
Height	10ft
Armament	7.62mm MG 42 machine gun
Weight	17 tonnes
Service Branch	Egyptian Marines

Saudi Arabia

M60

In the late 1970s, the Saudi Army had reinforced its armoured capability with more than 900 M60 main battle tanks. In 1990, Saudi Arabia inspected and purchased 390 newer M60A3s from US redundant resources. Tank crews were trained by the US Army and the 50-tonne armoured platforms were quickly integrated across the force. In the 1991 Gulf War, the Royal Saudi Army initially deployed several hundred tanks, which they later increased and operated throughout with the US Marines. Many of the Saudi M60s saw action as part of the Coalition force during the 1990–91 Gulf War and participated in the battle for Khafji.

The Battle of Khafji was the first major ground engagement of the Gulf War after the Iraq invasion and took place in and around the Saudi Arabian city of Khafju in late January 1991. The Iraqi leader had already tried and failed to draw Coalition forces into costly ground engagements by shelling Saudi Arabian positions and oil storage tanks and launching Scud surface-to-surface missiles at Israel. He ordered the invasion of Saudi Arabia from southern Kuwait. Iraqi Armoured Divisions were ordered to conduct a multi-pronged invasion towards Khafji, engaging Saudi Arabian, Kuwaiti and US forces along the coastline. The Iraqi divisions had suffered significant losses from attacks by Coalition aircraft in the preceding days. Most of their attacks were repulsed by the US forces, but one of the Iraqi columns occupied Khafji on the night of 29–30 January. Between 30 January and 1 February, two Saudi National Guard battalions and two Qatari tank companies attempted to retake control of the city, aided by Coalition aircraft and US artillery. By 1 February, the city had been recaptured at the cost of 43 Coalition servicemen dead and 52 wounded. Iraqi Army fatalities numbered between 60 and 300.

The M60 provided improved firepower, armoured protection, and range. It also had an advanced range finder and an integrated fire control system, making its firepower quicker and more accurate. The M60 incorporated the British-designed 105mm gun as its main gun and was able to destroy any known enemy tank. In post-war reviews, the M60s operated by the Saudis were found to have operated very well and the Saudis used them in attacks using 'manoeuvre warfare' tactics adopted by Western forces.

M60 Main Battle Tank Specification	
Model	M60 | upgraded M60A1 | M60A2 | M60A3
Manufacturer	Chrysler Corporation Delaware Defence Plant
Country	United States
Year	1960–subsequently upgraded in 1962, 1974 and 1979
Engine	Continental AVDS-1790 series turbo supercharged, fuel injection, 12-cylinder 750hp (559kW)
Fuel	Diesel
Protection	Cast homogeneous armour steel hull and turret with Kevlar lining
Top Speed	30mph (48km/h)
Range	310 miles (498km)
Crew Capacity	Four
Length	30ft
Width	12ft
Height	10ft
Armament	105mm M68 rifled gun, 7.62mm machine guns and .50 cal M85 heavy machine guns
Weight	50 tonnes
Service Branch	Saudi Arabia

AMX-30 Main Battle Tanks

In 1973, the Royal Saudi Army procured 190 AMX-30S main battle tanks. The S versions were simplified and adapted for desert combat. In 1979, the Saudis purchased another 100 variants. These tanks were mainly deployed with the 4th Saudi Armoured Brigade, which was structured and trained along French lines. It was equipped with 300 AMX-30 main battle tanks and 500 AMX-10P armoured infantry fighting vehicles, both French-made. Designed at the same time as the German Leopard, the AMX-30 was France's attempt to provide its armoured forces with a potent second-generation main battle tank,

Above: In 1990, Saudi Arabia inspected and purchased 390 M60A3s from US redundant resources. Tank crews were trained by the US Army. In the 1991 Gulf War, the Royal Saudi Army initially deployed several hundred tanks, adding more later and operating closely with the US Marines. (DPL)

Left: The M60 provided better firepower, armour protection, and range. It also had an advanced range finder and an integrated fire control system, making its firepower quicker and more accurate. The M60 incorporated the British-designed 105mm gun as its main gun and was able to destroy any known enemy tank. (DPL)

and the first French medium tank built since the late 1950s. Production of the AMX-30 began in 1966 at the Centre de Roanne and the AMX-30 was also built under licence in Spain. The hull of the AMX-30 is made of rolled steel plates welded together. The driver is seated at the front of the vehicle on the left with a single-piece hatch cover opening to the left and three periscopes. The centre periscope, depending on the model of the tank, may be a day periscope and can be replaced by an image-intensification night periscope. The other three crew members are seated in the turret, with the commander and gunner on the right and the loader, who also operates the radio, on the left. AMX-30 series MBTs were used by France, Saudi Arabia and Qatar during operations conducted early in 1991 to retake Kuwait following its invasion by Iraq in 1990. The French-equipped armoured brigade with AMX-30 was stationed at Tabuk in the northwest of Saudi Arabia and the brigade equipped with the United States M60s was at Khamis Mushayt in the southwest of the country.

AMX -30B Main Battle Tank Specification	
Model	AMX-30B Main Battle Tank – later upgraded to AMX-30 B2
Manufacturer	GIAT
Country	France
Year	1960s–retired 2023
Engine	Hispano-Suiza HS-110 multi-fuel
Fuel	Multi-fuel
Protection	Steel hull – 3in
Top Speed	40mph (64km/h)
Range	370 miles (595km)
Crew Capacity	Four
Length	31ft
Width	10ft
Height	7ft
Armament	105mm Modèle F1 Tank gun
Weight	36 tonnes
Service Branch	Saudi Arabia

Syria

T-62 Main Battle Tank

Syria had a long relationship with Czechoslovakian arms factories and in the early 1990s purchased the T-62 tank. It was regarded as a revolutionary tank at the time, with excellent armour protection, good manoeuvrability, and gun power. When it was first produced in 1961, it was undoubtedly the best main battle tank in the world but was quickly overtaken. The T-62 design was very low to the ground giving it a lower profile and making it harder to be hit. Unlike other tanks at the time, it was fitted with an autoloader, which was innovative and avoided the need for a loader who had to stand up – removing this member of the crew allowed the tank design to be lower. This system saves time and allows the gunner to locate a new target as the gun is being loader, but it requires ammunition to be stored alongside the crews. Grenade launchers fitted to the side of the turret could deploy smoke or white phosphorous to

The T-62 design was very low to the ground giving it a lower profile and making it harder to hit. Unlike other tanks of the time, it was fitted with an auto-loader. The T-62 also carried additional field drums at the rear. (DPL)

The three-man crews had to undertake specialist swimmer training, which included escaping from a flooded tank. Space was limited inside the tank; the gunner had very little room and the driver could hardly move away from his seated area. (DPL)

provide a screen to hide behind and in addition, the crew could vent diesel into the exhausts to generate a huge smoke screen. The three-man crews had to undertake specialist swimmer training, which included escaping from a flooded tank. Space was limited inside the tank; the gunner had very little room and the driver's seat area was cramped and very confined. The commander has the most room. Syria deployed 14,500 troops and several hundred tanks.

T-62 – Main Battle Tank Specification	
Model	T-62
Manufacturer	Soviet Union
Country	Origin design – Soviet Union
Year	1961–present
Engine	V-55V (based on the Kharkiv model V-2) 580hp (later 620)
Diesel	Diesel
Protection	Cast turret (242mm armour) 102mm front hull steel
Top Speed	31mph (50km/h)
Range	280 miles (450km)
Crew Capacity	Four
Length	3ft
Width	11ft
Height	8ft
Armament	115mm U-5TS (2A20) smoothbore gun
Weight	37 tonnes
Service Branch	Syrian Army

The T-62 was regarded as a world beater when it came into service. Its round turret could be confused with Iraqi Type 59 tanks from a distance. (US Army)

Other books you might like:

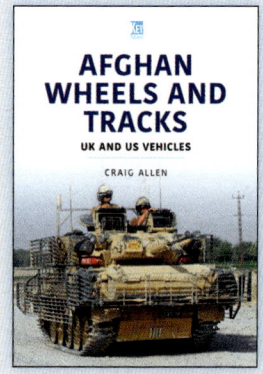
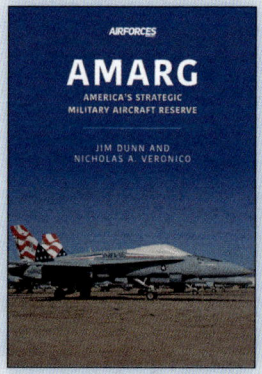
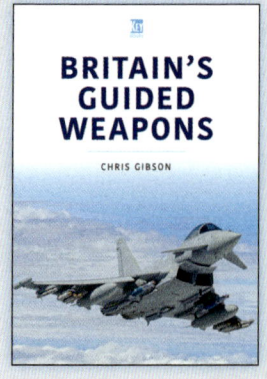
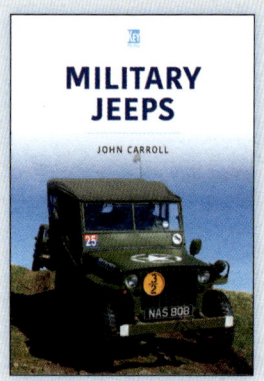

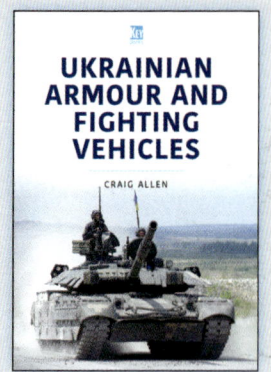

For our full range of titles please visit:
shop.keypublishing.com/books

VIP Book Club

Sign up today and receive
TWO FREE E-BOOKS

Be the first to find out about our forthcoming book releases and receive exclusive offers.

Register now at **keypublishing.com/vip-book-club**

Our VIP Book Club is a 100% spam-free zone, and we will never share your email with anyone else. You can read our full privacy policy at: privacy.keypublishing.com